Modern Dance
Twelve Creative Problem-Solving Experiments

Modern Dance

Twelve Creative Problem-Solving Experiments

Paulette Shafranski
California State University, Northridge

Scott, Foresman and Company
Glenview, Illinois   London, England

To my mother, whose love and understanding have provided me with the inspiration and the desire to create.

PREFACE

Modern Dance: Twelve Creative Problem-Solving Experiments is written to stimulate creativity and improvisation for the beginning student of modern dance while introducing the student to the skills needed to achieve meaningful self-expression through creative movement. The creative process as explored in the experiments that follow is a helpful means of discovering our own specific creative expressions in dance.

This book was written with a personal approach to an intriguing subject, creative problem solving in dance. I have taken the liberty to touch that small part of each of us that calls on us to move and to express ourselves creatively in movement, specifically in dance. What we intend to say in movement and how we express ourselves is unique to each of us. Our birthright is to become expressive to the point that we can harmonize our internal yearnings with external movement, in this case, dance.

Part 1 of this workbook explores the role of creativity and imagination in dance and introduces the goals of the twelve problem-solving experiments that follow.

The twelve experiments in Part 2 provide both students of dance and dance instructors with guidelines for developing small dance studies. The first six experiments are organized to help students begin developing an understanding of time, and a better awareness of space, energy, and concentration. The next three experiments are designed to help students appreciate movement and the feelings and meaning it has the potential to convey. Finally, after encouraging the student to develop greater self-awareness and control of a variety of movements, the last three experiments help students—either as individuals or in groups—realize a small, creative dance composition of their own design and perform it with confidence.

Each of the twelve experiments is organized in the following way: first, the goal of the experiment is identified; second, the problem that the experiment addresses is indicated; finally, the process to be followed to meet that goal is presented. The process is presented as exercises and guidelines that convey the information essential to solving the problem, but that allow students to adapt the skills and awareness they have developed in the most creative ways possible. Throughout these exercises, questions to the student appear in italics beside the space for the student's written response. This workbook is perforated so that the student can complete exercises and respond to questions, tear out the relevant pages, and turn them in to the instructor for comments.

Finally, in Part 3, the student is encouraged to review the creative problem-solving process to develop the skills of self-examination that are necessary to attain high levels of achievement and to enhance self-expression.

Expressing ourselves is the desire. To reach out and communicate with each other is the aim. That is what the creative impulse, within us, is all about. This creative impulse has no designee for any age, but exists for all ages. This impulse is awaiting expression and nourishment in the very old as well as the very young.

At the heart of each individual is the desire to be discovered and understood. The creative impulse reaches out to make the human connection possible through movement. This special creative act is the natural desire to dance.

Although you will be able to read this book in a short period of time, you will discover that each problem requires time and attention to explore completely. This time allows your own experimentation to unfold in movement, in dance, and in life.

ACKNOWLEDGMENTS

I wish to express my sincere appreciation to Dr. Tillman Hall, a person who "believes," and to Virginia White for her helpfulness in preparing the manuscript.

Sincere love and respect are expressed to the many dedicated teachers and devoted students who have enriched my life.

Paulette Shafranski

Contents

PART ONE
An Introduction: Exploring the Dance

The Creative Impulse

The creative impulse is the spontaneous desire to produce something outside of ourselves so we can experience it as a form of expression and accomplishment.

As we live we create constant challenges to discover and grow to stimulate our linkage with ourselves, others, and our world.

Growing creatively must not be underestimated. It is a powerful force in our own life. The force of life is energy. Our body processes this flow of energy, which is self-fulfilling or empty, depending on our relationship to the self. In the creative impulse we fuse with this energetic self; we get in touch with *what* we are trying to express and accomplish. Everyone alive is trying to do something, to create a mood, an idea, an ambition, or an action.

This desire to produce something, to ignite the internal forces and move out to externalize itself in some way, is the creative impulse.

In dance, this creative impulse manifests itself in desiring to move and accomplishing that movement.

Creative energy is life-sustaining. It can propel our lives forward—it can make sense out of chaos—by stimulating order and design and by searching to uncover the eternal mysteries that range from self to the destiny of humankind.

A BEGINNING

Understanding the creative impulse in movement and the study thereof is a valuable process. We can make a small beginning when we discover that we possess a bodily instrument that is a moving force of life, occupying space and energizing itself in time.

The time we have with each other can be greatly enhanced when we allow ourselves the right to explore the creative potential of our own phenomenal instrument.

The experiments, as outlined in Part 2 of this workbook, deal primarily with problem-solving experiences in creative movement. Therefore one is advised to approach these experiments in such a way as to include specific techniques in body placement prior to these experiences. Each experiment touches on one or more of the specific aspects of movement exploration. The experiments lead the creator into personal dance discoveries.

The *kinesthetic sense,* which will be explored in the first experiment, is available to us when we concentrate on our own movement possibilities. Remembering those given movements and translating those feelings into body positions and movement patterns within the body is the process. Remembering sequences of movement gives us the confidence to *repeat* and *restructure* patterns to organize our level of creative discovery in dance.

PROBLEM SOLVING

The problem-solving method used in this workbook involves a two-step process. First, there is a specific creative problem stated in each experiment. Second, the student is asked to solve the problem to the best of his or her present ability.

The problem allows each person a framework to work within so that a given problem can be solved. The thinking process is very important. When an individual is confronted with a problem, he or she has something specific to achieve. These limitations enhance meeting the challenge of stretching the mind to meet that creative activity at hand. The results are creative movement responses as posed by the problem. These problem-solving experiences can allow for a rich exchange of creative thinking and creative movement exploration.

The twelve experiments are meant to be a creative growth stimulus. This approach is just a beginning to the depth of the creative problem-solving approach. This method is a never ending source of unique activity. Each individual is given an opportunity to develop in movement exploration.

PRIMARY CREATIVE PROBLEM-SOLVING OBJECTIVE

The primary objective is to create an environment whereby each individual will be allowed to experience and explore the phenomenal act of constant discovery of movement in the creative problem-solving process as it relates to dance. Objectives in the creative, problem-solving challenge to consider are the:

Vision to see movement differently

Joy of discovering new and old movements

Opportunity to experience being sensitive, aware, alive, and open for movement changes

Inspiration to recognize the pure movement experience as a means of communication and expression

Attitudes in a sharing environment that stimulate creativity include:

Mutual respect

Mutual support

Self-confidence

Observed silences

Encouragement

Constructive criticism

Open attitude toward success and failure

Sense of accomplishment

Compassion

Inspiration

A positive, constructive attitude is essential in creating an environment of trust and quality. Destructive aspects must be rejected in every way. The exploring environment and that environment extended into daily life is emphasized so that appreciative, sensitive people are developed.

An atmosphere of individual acceptance is important for the creative process to take place. Everyone needs to feel comfortable to experience both success and failure as the process unfolds.

In the space provided, write your brief answers to the following questions.

What is a creative attitude?   ....

....

....

....

What is the creative problem-solving method?   ....

....

....

....

Discuss your answers in a sharing situation. Establish a community spirit among your fellow participants. The "spirit of the place" can be established the very first day that you and your group are together; maintaining the mutual respect that you establish early will later help you deal with the openness and vulnerability that you will share later.

GOALS IN UNDERTAKING THE PROCESS OF CREATIVITY

1. Set the working atmosphere for openness.
2. Stimulate the mind so that an energizing atmosphere exists.
3. Observe and be sensitive to each other so that the creative activity will unfold.
4. Motivate self and others in pursuit of the mutual "gift" of discovery, and allow the process to happen.
5. Be aware of a final sense of wholeness and closure.

EXPLORING THE DANCE

Every day we embark on an adventure, one that we have been on each day of our lives. This adventure is that of seeing and sensing movement.

We, as creatures of movement, transport ourselves daily in our environment, yet we often take these moving abilities for granted.

When we attempt to analyze what we are all about, we realize that movement is the nature of our own aliveness. When we move in our world we feel alive and present.

If we search we will find our own form of *aliveness* in creating the dance. Our dance-life movement is the very essence of our own movement reaction to the social, pyschological environment. We dance as children moving with rhythm in a dance-life form as we respond to music either sung or played. We hear that hypnotic beat, we feel that sense of oneness, and we reach to hang on to the pulse of our being.

The first dance as a child appears to be bouncing up and down and around and about. With it comes a smile and arm gestures that balance the body in action in space. Oh! what a state of joy. Often the end is a fall to the floor or a run to out-reached arms of a parent, relative, or person enjoying this ritual of living.

Why do we choose to dance? Is it an instinctive activity? Is it a way of communicating? Is it a way of moving? It is, we know, a celebration of life.

Since we *all* have enjoyed such an experience early on, we will assume that it is one of nature's ways of personal expression. This natural dance is spontaneous and full of untold enthusiasm. It has a feeling of being free and full of energy. It is our childlike statement, "I am alone moving for the joy of it!"

As we travel through our various stages of development we often lose these spontaneous and enthusiastic movements. We do establish extended dance-like states with groups of people in social dance and sport, but when it comes to our personal spontaneity we often feel awkward, and respond with inhibition and lack of understanding of that which was once instantaneous and fresh as a child.

In this journey of movement exploration we will take ourselves back to those natural movements by closely observing that natural dance-like activity of the child within us. When we observe we give ourselves the opportunity to visit our past and reflect on our own beginnings in dance-like forms.

Let us begin today to see, to sense, and to know movement through our own observation. By studying movement within and outside of our own body we will come to understand our own remarkable instrument. Let us begin to explore the dance together.

EXPLORING DANCE

The following pages are filled with descriptive words about dance. These words can begin to stimulate us and fill our imaginations as we reflect upon what dance movement means to us. These isolated thoughts can begin to reach our creative thinking process by freely associating action, movement, and ideas that exist in our daily life. Our personal association to our own thoughts is the beginning of igniting our internal creative forces so necessary for looking at and finding meanings in our moving world. Consider the following interpretations of what dance can mean to some people.

DANCE IS

SHAPE of line

COLOR of emotion

FORM of the body

TIME of day

DIRECTION of motion

SPACE we occupy

ENERGY that changes

LEVELS of ideas

DYNAMICS of action

COMMUNICATION of people

INVOLVEMENT of others

IMAGES of ideas

DESIGNS of lines

LIFE of self

BREATHING in air

STILLNESS of silence

TRAVELING in space

MOTION of action

BEAUTY of nature

RHYTHM of the heart

ART of the third dimension

MOVEMENT of people

FREEDOM of expression

THERAPY for sadness

EXPRESSION of joy

FUN of exploration

CREATIVE and real

EXCITING and energetic

DIFFICULT as understanding

IMAGINATIVE and powerful

JOY of living

PAIN of strength

FRUSTRATION of knowing

WORKING to achieve

Fill in your own thoughts to add to the words below, and relate them to your own ideas on dance.

DANCE IS

DESIRABLE ....

BELIEVABLE ....

POSITIONS ....

COMPLETE ....

SIMPLISTIC ....

ACTION ....

EXACT ....

YOU ....

ME ....

COMMUNION ....

COSMIC ....

PERFORMING ....

ECSTASY ....

What can dance do for us?

DANCE CAN

RELEASE anxieties

BRING people together

BRING ABOUT a sense of harmony

ALLOW us to express ourselves

GIVE us added pleasure

SHOW our emotions

MAKE us happy

RELEASE energy

CONTAIN energy

PROVIDE entertainment

RELEASE inhibitions

RELEASE creativity

STRENGTHEN our bodies

STRENGTHEN our discipline

COORDINATE our own bodily movements

HEIGHTEN our awareness of form

DEVELOP creativity

AID in communicating with others

IMPROVE our motor memory

OPEN our intuitive mind

DEVELOP kinesthetic techniques

Add to the list any ideas you would like to express.

....

....

....

....

DANCE IS

A means of communicating

An intense expression of emotion

A natural high

Allowing the inner being to come out

A mind and body relationship

Moving through life's experiences

A way of dreaming

Letting go of inner tensions

Taking yourself to another place in time

MODERN DANCE

Modern dance is a unique form of self-expression. The dancer's body is the instrument through which all of the human movement expressions are utilized to give way to the dance. Modern dance is unique. It has no given structure as does ballet. Modern dance has excitement, drama, emotional color, rhythm, spatial design, energy changes, and continual surprises. It is no surprise, therefore, to find each modern dancer in each era or decade to be uniquely his or her own person possessing unique ways of expressing themselves.

Modern dance involves our own personal discovery of movement. We make the creative aspects of the dance live for us when we explore the creative problem-solving aspects of space, time, and energy as they relate to the dance. Dance is . . . you.

ASSIGNMENT

Design a series of personal discovery statements that describe what dance is. Begin each statement with the words *Dance is . . . .*

1. ....

....

2. ....
....

3. ....
....

4. ....
....

5. ....
....

PART TWO
Twelve Creative Problem-Solving Experiments in Modern Dance

1

An Experiment in Personal Discovery
≪ *THE KINESTHETIC SENSE* ≫

The basic five senses include seeing, hearing, smelling, tasting, and touching. The *kinesthetic sense* is the sixth sense. The kinesthetic sense is the sense of knowing where we are in relation to the self (a muscle sense) a sense of movement within our own body. This sense of movement within our own body includes our inner awareness of our own relationship to space, energy, and size of movement. The body senses itself in space. It reacts to the sensation of nerve endings as they respond to the muscle structure of the body. This inner awareness of where we are in relation to the body as it exists in space gives us the kinesthetic sense, the sense of our own body movement within itself.

The kinesthetic sense is a movement sense utilized by a dancer's every move. If we close our eyes we can experience one of the joys of our own movement as we explore this idea. For example, close your eyes and stretch out your arms to the extreme right and left side, at shoulder level. Now slowly move your two index fingers toward each other in front of you. The two index fingers will find each other through the kinesthetic sense of your own movement within your body. The kinesthetic sense is that sense of being able to respond to a series of complex movements moving to bring those two fingers together. We rely on the kinesthetic experience to appreciate and know our own movements in our daily life.

In the creative, problem-solving process we will be constantly concerned with the kinesthetic sense. This sense gives us the ability to feel relationships in space and translate those moving impulses into designs and shapes in movement. Our natural movements are the original source and substance of the dance experience.

In the following experiment in the kinesthetic discovery we will experience the positions of sleep as an original creative experience. The body can be understood as the supreme creative form.

KINESTHETIC PERSONAL DISCOVERY: NATURAL SLEEPING POSITIONS

Let's concentrate on a simple initial idea—that of finding your own natural positions for sleep. Take the time to find your daily sleeping positions and select those most comfortable. Study these positions and be able to relate to them in your own body design. Take mental notes or make sketches to define the pattern of the body. Learn to kinesthetically sense each form, and draw on paper the respective shapes if necessary.

Take the time to recreate these forms and repeat these positions several times in order to understand them. Allow yourself to consciously remember the practiced movements. Your own original style of sleeping is unique to you. Your body tells you what feels comfortable. Your choice is your own creative drive to fall asleep. Your natural positions give you the confidence to kinesthetically find your own way.

Drawings even on a primitive level can allow you to visualize the positions and note the details and help you recreate and remember the moment. This is a slow but disciplined method. This same experiment can be done with one person as the performer and another as the observer. These observations can then be noted; for example, making written notes of the body's position, or lying on the abdomen, right side of the face on the floor, left hand over head, and so on. An observed description helps to identify the process. This process will be slow at first, involving the importance of intense kinesthetic concentration.

Our personal kinesthetic discovery is as simple as recognizing our natural positions for sleep as a moving form of a natural dance.

EXPERIMENT 1

Personal Discovery
THE KINESTHETIC SENSE

Description This is an experiment in discovering the kinesthetic sense and applying it to the memory of our own movements.

Problem Create a study that has three or four sleeping positions, then move slowly from one position to the next without stopping.

Process Study your own positions that you find desirable for sleeping. Concentrate and memorize three of these positions. Now, through your careful selection, move naturally, in slow motion from one position to the next.

Evaluation Each individual can select a partner to work with in a cooperative spirit. The aim is to help each other to be precise in memorizing these moving positions. Practice these combinations until they become absolutely automatic, and you will be aware of the element of having a motor memory.

Suggestions The final sequences will be shown in front of the group as solo statements. The sleeping postures will be visually stimulating to watch in slow movement—a moving moment shared and remembered.

An Experiment in Movement
≪ *LOCOMOTOR AND NONLOCOMOTOR MOVEMENT* ≫

In modern dance we can use all of our natural movements as the source and substance of our dancing vocabulary. Movement can be utilized in so many ways. We move to communicate; we move to go somewhere; we move to express ourselves. We move out of the need to relate to others in order to give and to receive.

We achieve a sense of movement and its variety of meanings in dance when we begin to analyze what we and others are doing. In dance we select movement; our selection is limited or extended depending on our experience, explorations, and training.

In the beginning of our life we learned to move in a number of unique ways in order to get from one place to another. The pre-walking stage involved creeping, crawling, sliding, slithering, and so forth. In order to stand, we stretched, pulled, grasped, clasped, balanced, and stood. As we progressed, we walked, ran, skipped, jumped, fell, turned, whirled, floated, and moved in intriguing ways to discover ourselves, our environment, our friends, relatives, nature, and the importance of play.

All of the above movement created our life situation allowing us mobility and the joy of moving, which was and is still filled with discovery. We can become gatherers of movement when we study movement both by observation and participation in the moving experience. We begin to compose when we relate those observations and experiences and create unique movement combinations of our own.

In dance we like to analyze what we have done and what we are doing so that we can structure our dance movement into remembered phrases and eventually into dance compositions. Locomotor and nonlocomotor movements are two general categories that help us define and analyze movement in dance.

LOCOMOTOR MOVEMENT

What is *locomotor* movement? Locomotor movement is movement traveling through space. There are eight common traveling movements.

Even Rhythm	*Uneven Rhythm*
Walk	Slide
Run	Skip
Jump	Gallop
Hop	
Leap	

Any locomotor movement can be combined with any of the other locomotor movements to make interesting and varied movement combinations. For the sake of simplicity, let's concentrate on these eight basic locomotor movements. Remember them and create a number of new and unique locomotor combinations.

Walk The walk is performed by transferring weight alternately from one foot to the other. This locomotor movement is the most common. The walk has an even rhythm.

Run The run is accomplished by an equal transfer of weight from one foot to another. Between each step is a suspended motion produced by pushing off from the ball of one foot to the other. The body is leaning forward in a forward run. The arms are normally in opposition to the feet to create balance in motion. The run is even in rhythm.

Jump A jump requires the body to lift off from the floor from one or both feet. The most common jump is produced by pushing off from both feet simultaneously. When the jump is in the air, both legs and feet are extended. When landing, the feet are cushioned by the balls of the feet with legs and ankles flexed. The jump can also be performed by pushing off from one foot and landing on both feet. The jump is even in rhythm.

Hop The hop requires a push-off from the floor from one foot and landing on the same foot. The push-off and the landing require the leg to be flexed. When the hop is in the air, that leg is fully extended. The opposite leg can be placed in a variety of positions, perhaps in a flexion or an extension. The hop is also even in rhythm.

Leap The leap is performed by pushing off from one foot and landing on the alternate foot. The body is temporarily suspended in the air between the push-off and the landing. The simple leap is executed with both legs extended at the moment of suspension. Variations include one or the other knee being flexed (or both while in the air). Combine with walking, runs, and steps to produce periods of rest. A leap by itself is even in rhythm.

Slide The slide is performed in an uneven rhythm pattern—long-short, repeat, long-short. The foot pattern has two parts; for example, if the right foot leads as the step and the left foot follows with a closing gliding step, the foot has contact with the floor (repeat). The slide itself is steady and smooth in quality as it progresses across the floor.

Skip The skip is created by combining the movement of a step followed by a hop. The rhythm is uneven long-short. The skip can also be performed with the up-beat-hop-step; then the rhythm is short-long and is also uneven (arms support the body best in opposition).

Gallop The gallop has two steps performed in an uneven rhythm pattern; long-short-long-short. One foot leads and the other foot follows with a cut step; repeat to create a pattern. For example, lead step begins by stepping on the right foot with a bent knee and pushes off into the air extended recovering on the left foot with a bent knee repeat.

NONLOCOMOTOR MOVEMENT

The nonlocomotor movement includes movement that does not travel through space. What is *axial* movement? Axial movement is considered nonlocomotor. Axial movement can be a whole or partial turn of the body. Axial movement is also movement that occurs in utilizing any of the various joints of the body. Bending, stretching, twisting, turning, swaying, pushing, pulling, or rotating any of the body parts (for example, arms, legs, head, or torso) are axial movements.

Movement, such as falling and recovering, is also included in this category. Falls can occur from several levels and can therefore be explored from a variety of positions such as standing, kneeling, sitting, etc. The fall can be a complete or partial fall to the floor. The whole or any part of the body can be involved in creating a fall.

Nonlocomotor movements can be performed in one place or they can be combined with locomotor movement that travels and moves throughout space.

MOVEMENT

How we move and why we move is definitely a theme weaving in and around the dance. In dance we can move and look at the pure pleasure of moving. We can do two jumps, three runs, stop, execute a small turn, and fall to the floor. Another interesting way of looking at movement is to become familiar with the daily motivations for moving. Our own observations then become another source for finding movement. Once we find the movement and the motivation for moving, we can begin to explore the new dancing vocabulary in a variety of ways.

EXPLORING NEW MOVEMENT

Finding new movement is a joy, a source of great pleasure and a necessity in dance. Through daily observation, look for specific locomotor movements and add your findings to the following list of the eight basic locomotor movements with their corresponding motivations.

Walking
For pleasure
To work
In a hurry
With a child
With an elderly person

Running
To escape from fire
In a race
For exercise
On a beach
To cross a street

Jumping
For joy
In a game of volleyball
Out of bed
In aerobics

Hopping
Someone stepped on your toes
Playing a game
Hopscotch

Leaping
Over water
Over a hurdle

Sliding   As in a folk dance
As through a narrow passage

Skipping   For pleasure
Rope

Galloping   In the act of play
As horses do

EXPLORING GAMES

Games are a natural mix of locomotor and axial movements. For example, baseball and hopscotch involve a variety of movement:

Baseball   Running, throwing, swinging, bending, falling, recovering

Hopscotch   Hopping, jumping, twisting, turning, reaching

Add to the list other games that include locomotor and axial movement:

Game   *Movement*

1. ....

....

2. ....

....

EXPLORING LOCOMOTOR AND AXIAL MOVEMENTS

Locomotor movements can be changed in so many ways:

Walk
Run
Leap   As fast as you can
Jump   As slow as you can
Hop   As large as you can
Skip   As small as you can
Gallop
Slide

Taking natural movement and exploring the possibilities of change can produce surprising results. Changing the natural into exaggerated or diminished forms, or changing the speed of the movement is the beginning of learning abstraction. Abstraction can be defined as changing the way in which a movement is performed, but the essence of the movement is still there.

Axial movements can also be explored and changed in a similar way:

Bend
Twist
Turn
Rotate   As fast as you can
Push   As slow as you can
Pull   As large as you can
Stretch   As small as you can
Sway
Fall

EXPLORING MOVEMENT COMBINATIONS

Before you make your own movement combinations, consider the following examples:

1. Using any of the eight locomotor movements—walking, running, hopping, jumping, skipping, sliding, leaping, and galloping—make a combination of any three.
2. Using axial movements—bending, twisting, turning, swaying, rotating, pushing, pulling, and falling—make a combination of any two.

MASTERING SPECIFIC MOVEMENT COMBINATIONS

1. Four jumps, forward, back, right, and left. Right foot slide and lunge.
   Suggestion: Rearrange the way these movements are put together.
2. Eight-count walk to the right in a circle; diagonal run for eight counts; freeze for two with an added six-count right arm swing.
   Suggestion: Use twenty-four counts utilizing running, walking, freezing, and a right-arm swing. Create your own variation.

3. Walk for three counts—execute two skips for two counts; turn for three counts.
   Suggestion: Skip for two counts, walk for two, execute three skips and one step; create any number of changes—whenever and however you wish.

Make two new suggested movement combinations using any movement you wish:

1. ....

....

....

2. ....

....

....

MOVEMENT IN SLOW MOTION

Slow motion allows us the time to study and learn the art of moving in a slow, continuous, and concentrated way. When we move slowly, we can study motion and deliberately control each move. This method allows us the time to articulate each movement no matter how small.

We slow down movement to secure the action second-by-second; when this movement is repeated, we then have control over the very essence of each moving moment. Slow motion allows us the opportunity to explore the strength of our own control.

To control movement consciously we give ourselves the privilege of knowing exactly what we are doing. This observed and projected knowledge gives us the ability to repeat, recreate, and restructure any given movement because we have perceived it and know it kinesthetically in the moving body.

Through this knowledge we can enjoy each moving moment. We begin to master each move by slowing down the motion and disciplining the self to acquire patience. The ability to comprehend and translate the movement as we are perceiving it can be considered reading the kinesthetic moment.

EXPERIMENT 2

Movement
LOCOMOTOR AND NONLOCOMOTOR MOVEMENT

Description   This is an experiment in using slow motion as a way of understanding the axial and locomotor movements of another person.

Problem   Create a study that involves two movement statements—*A* and *B*—involving twenty-four counts (twelve counts each).

Process   One person is selected as *A,* another is *B.* When *A* begins, the statement will utilize both axial and locomotor movements, ending with a movement to the floor. When *B's* movement is composed, it will begin on the floor and will be developed with *axial* and *locomotor movements* that will end standing. (Work out the problems separately.) The *A* person and the *B* person now each have twelve counts. Combine the movements of *A* and *B,* and learn each other's movement pattern. We now have twenty-four counts.

Evaluation   Each individual in the *A* and *B* combination can then watch each other and enjoy the other person's movement pattern. Each person can appreciate what the other has done (twelve separate counts each). A second group of *A* and *B* can evaluate how well the first group of *A* and *B* accomplishes their movement statements in slow motion. The *A* and *B* can be executed using unison and full twenty-four counts, each performing each other's movement to complete *A* and *B* in unison.

Suggestions   The two groups of *A* and *B* can join each other and complete a forty-eight count movement pattern. If the group is satisfied with the unison experience, they will be able to slow up or increase speed to change this experiment into a dynamic moving experience. Control is essential.

An Experiment in Time

≪ *RHYTHM* ≫

Time is a self-perpetuating continuum, for time is also movement in the eternal sense. We use time to regulate and give order to our lives. Life has a sense of a beginning, middle, and end because of it.

In dance, we refer to time as the interval between the opening and closing. The life of a small creative piece in dance, therefore, can be a life situation in miniature. We can develop anything in dance and make it short- or long-lived, depending on how we wish to develop the time-line idea.

Time is so unique it is always passing by. How can we catch it, secure it, and make it work for us within the structure of movement/life and the dance? Let's think of time as ever present, ever moving, and ever being.

We can further divide time into seconds until we can present a complete minute. Recognizing a minute is easy—we see minutes passing by each day on clocks and in our daily lives. Those minutes make hours and lifetimes. A minute has a beginning, a middle, and an end. Imagine this: The beginning is 1001, the middle is 1030, and the end 1060. Everything in the middle between 1001–1060 helps fill out the plan of one minute. We can have someone stand in the middle of a room and give us the downbeat of that minute with a stopwatch and at sixty seconds give us the end of that minute in time. Thus we have experienced that very minute in time. We have in essence waited for it to happen. Now let us explore what can occur in the following examples.

List what can occur in a few seconds in life:

1. ....

2. ....

3. ....

4. ....

5. ....

List what can occur in a minute in a life situation:

1. ....

2. ....

3. ....

4. ....

5. ....

By thinking about what can and does occur in a life situation in seconds or minutes, we can begin to react to life and its value in time, and relate the life situations to the dance experience.

Time can be the duration of a dance. Time can be seconds, minutes, hours, and lifetimes. Time can be divided into the rate of speed being fast, moderate, or slow. Time can be the rhythm in music. Time is the time we have together; the time we have apart. Time is short, time is long. Time is eternal. Time doesn't exist. Time is the meter of music. Time is divided. Time is stressed. Time is important. Time needs to be understood so we can control time in the framework of a dance.

Time is also the underlying rhythmic sense of the dance. In the beginning we can sense time by our own internal heartbeat. This inner pulse gives us the sense of our own duration in time which is life.

In dance, there is a musical duration called rhythm, which holds our living dance piece together. To understand time and rhythm, we must understand the basis of music; the beats are the essential elements necessary to understand the marriage of dance and rhythm.

Rhythm is notated so that it can be read, understood, and played. The dancer must understand how a piece of music is organized so that the dancer can be knowledgeable about beats, musical form, and structure.

MUSICAL NOTES

How long a note is sounded, how long it lasts, is determined by its *value*. The relative value or duration of a note is relative to other notes. The relative values of five different notes are listed below.

Whole Note

𝐨

Half Note   Two half notes = one whole note.

𝅗𝅥 𝅗𝅥

Quarter Note   Four quarter-notes = one whole note.

♩ ♩ ♩ ♩

Eighth Note   Eight eighth-notes = one whole note.

Sixteenth Note   Sixteen sixteenth-notes = one whole note.

METER

The *meter* of music is the recurring rhythmic pattern of the music, a pattern that is grouped in *measures.* A measure is the unit we use to divide the pulse, the rhythm, the beats of music. Think of meter as the basic pattern of beats per measure.

TIME SIGNATURE

The *time signature,* usually expressed as a fraction at the beginning of a measure, tells, first, what kind of note is taken as the time unit for the beat, and, second, how many of them can be in a measure. The following is an example of two measures of music in $\frac{2}{4}$ (read "two-quarter") time.

In music the time signature has two numbers, for example, $\frac{2}{4}$. The top number indicates the number of beats per measure, and the bottom number indicates which note gets a value of one. In the two measures marked $\frac{2}{4}$, the time signature indicates $\frac{2}{4}$ time: the upper number indicates two beats per measure, or any note value equaling two counts; the lower number indicates that the quarter-note equals a value of one.

If you were to sound out the notes in the two measures described above, you could say, "one, two, one-and-two-and." If you take the same amount of time to say "one-and-two-and" as you take to say "one, two," then you're counting out the rhythm of these two bars correctly.

The following are examples of other measures of music in $\frac{2}{4}$ time, which also show the relative values of notes when there are only two beats per measure. (The sixteenth notes in the fourth measure are counted out as "one-ee-and-da, two-ee-and-da" to help you understand the rhythm.)

Create your own four measures in $\frac{2}{4}$ time:

The numbers 1 & 2 &, etc., do not usually appear beneath measures of music, but are included here to help remind you of the beat underlying each measure. These notes are arranged with three beats per measure:

Create your own four measures in ¾ time:

These notes are arranged with four beats per measure:

Create your own four measures in $\frac{4}{4}$ time:

These notes are arranged in six measures with five beats per measure:

Create your own four measures in $\frac{5}{4}$ time.

The time signature of $\frac{3}{8}$ indicates that there are three beats per measure and the eighth-note gets a value of one. There are *three beats per measure* in each of the following:

Create your own four measures in $\frac{3}{8}$ time.

$\frac{3}{8}$ | | | |

The following notes are arranged with six beats per measure. The numbers below them now show each of the six beats.

Create your own four measures in $\frac{6}{8}$ time. Although the numbers are not printed below the measures, remember that there are six beats per measure.

$\frac{6}{8}$ | | | |

RHYTHMIC DEVICES

Mixed Meters   *Mixed meters* is in essence changing the meters. For example, mixing the meters using $\frac{1}{4}$, $\frac{2}{4}$, and $\frac{3}{4}$ time, we have

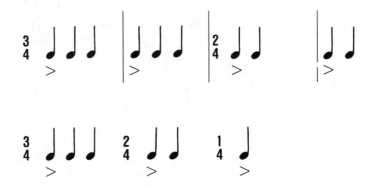

Notice that some of the meters have two measures of the same time signature before changing.

Create your own mixed meter rhythm pattern using the following meters: $\frac{1}{4}$, $\frac{2}{4}$, $\frac{3}{4}$, $\frac{4}{4}$, $\frac{5}{4}$, $\frac{6}{4}$, and $\frac{7}{4}$.

Accumulative and Decumulative Meters

Accumulative meters means adding to each measure as you increase the number of beats corresponding to the time signature. Decumulative meters means decreasing in number of beats per measure corresponding to the time signature.

Accumulative Meter

Decumulative Meter

Accumulative and Decumulative Meter

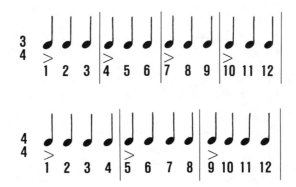

Resultant Rhythm

Combining two meters simultaneously by adding two phrases produces the resultant rhythm. Using $\frac{3}{4}$ and $\frac{4}{4}$ rhythms, for example, we have:

The resultant rhythm is:

Syncopation Syncopation means changing the accent (which exists on the count of one) to another beat or beats in a measure.

Normal accent

Syncopated

EXPERIMENT

Time
RHYTHM

Description   This is an experiment in understanding rhythm structures and how to combine and mix meters.

Problem   On a separate sheet of paper, create a study that has mixed meter so that your total count is twenty-four.

Process   Select a new meter for each measure or repeat any measure using $\frac{1}{4}$, $\frac{2}{4}$, $\frac{3}{4}$, and $\frac{4}{4}$ time signatures.

       With each new time signature select a new movement, either locomotion or axial or any combination of the two, to give the mixed meter excitement. Accent the downbeat of each measure.

Evaluation   Find another individual; sit down and discuss the measures and meters. Check the twenty-four count study in terms of the mixed meters and the changing movements. Did you accomplish the movement change with the introduction of each new time signature? Were the movements and meters clear to the observer?

Suggestions   Take both scores of the mixed meter in movement form and perform the work in front of class.

An Experiment in Space

≪ LEVELS, DIRECTION, AND DIMENSION ≫

Space is all around us. We occupy space; we move in space; we design space; we conquer space; and we divide space.

In dance, space is what the dancer occupies, moves in and through. The dancer in space has level, stage direction, floor pattern, spatial designs, dimension, and focus.

To understand the design of dance further, we also need to recognize symmetry and asymmetry. These varied aspects of space are important in the structuring of a dance. When we shape the dance in space, all of the above elements are at work. The importance of space and how to control space is included in the following descriptions:

LEVEL

The design our body makes in space exists on three basic levels. They are:

High   Middle   Low

One can further divide the levels into:

High   High Middle   Middle   Middle Low   Low

Suggested examples:

Low   Sleeping on the floor
Slithering or rolling on the floor

Low Middle   Crawling on all fours
Sitting on the floor
Kneeling

Middle　Standing
Walking
Running
Standing turn

Middle High　Sliding
Galloping
Skipping

High　Jumping
Body Lifts
Leaping high

All of the categories of high, middle, and low are relative to the total shape of the spatial movement. These possibilities are suggested to be explored and enjoyed.

Low—On the ground
Middle—Between ground and air
High—Reaching and/or gaining altitude

Explore other possibilities and try to categorize movement, both axial and locomotive, for each level. Some movements travel through all three levels in a short period of time.

STAGE DIRECTIONS

The space the dancer dances in can be thought of as a stage. Stage directions are important, for they give the dancer a relationship to the audience. The stage directions shown here are from the dancer's point of view as the dancer faces the audience.

AUDIENCE

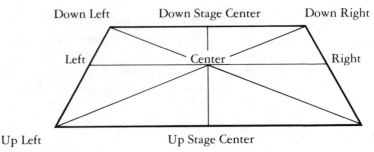

In stage space:

> *Forward* (Downstage) is toward the audience
> *Backward* (Upstage) is away from the audience
> *Right Side* (Stage Right) is to the dancer's right
> *Left Side* (Stage Left) is to the dancer's left
> *Diagonal Lines* reach the four corners of the stage
> *Center* is the middle of the stage where all lines intersect

The stage is a dancing space. The dancer's space can be a theatre, a studio, a park, a garden. Wherever the dancer dances, it is important to establish where the dancer is in relation to the audience.

EXPLORING STAGE SPACE

To explore the stage space, create some spontaneous action. For example,

> Wherever you are, run to center stage.
> All walk diagonally downstage, right.
> Face upstage left and skip through center to upstage left.

Create your own suggestions and have others follow your directions.

1. ....

2. ....

3. ....

Floor Pattern
The dancer's floor pattern is a design created as a result of moving from place to place. Simple spatial floor patterns would be a circle, a diagonal line, a zigzag, concentric circles, a semicircle, a series of angle lines—the combinations are many.

Spatial Design
Your body has a three-dimensional quality as you move in space either on a horizontal or vertical plane. Because your body exists as a moving pattern in space, you will be making spatial designs with your body as you cut through space.

The spatial body design has a design pattern in space that includes the negative and positive space, as shown in Part 1 of Experiment 4.

Symmetry and Asymmetry

Symmetry and asymmetry are two shapes that a dancer is concerned with when designing movement. Symmetry means that both sides of the design are equal and balanced. Asymmetry means that the design is unbalanced (both sides are unequal and lacking balance).

Symmetry can be orderly, harmonious, and deadly. Asymmetry can be exciting, dynamic, stimulating, and free.

AXIAL SPATIAL DESIGNS

The spatial design also can be considered as a rotating space pattern around a basic 360°. The axial body, therefore, is a design that exists on a base rotating around 360°. The directions the body moves in can be thought of this way:

Forward 0° or 360°
Backward 180°
Right 90°
Left 270°
Diagonal down right 45°
Diagonal up left 225°
Diagonal down left 315°
Diagonal up right 135°

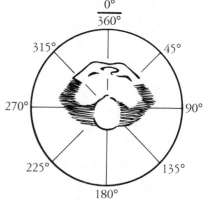

Circle Axial Design

The body, in an axial design, is the center itself. The relative base allows the body to move in these directions in ways around itself with the body limitation, as the examples in Experiment 4 will show.

DIMENSION

The dimension of body movement is considered the size or the range of the move or movement itself. For example,

Waving with your fingers, an abstraction.
Decreased dimension—small
Waving in a normal way (hand and lower arm)
Normal dimension—medium
Waving in an exaggerated way (shoulder and upper body)—
enlarging the movement
Increased dimension—large

Note the range of motion in the above three examples allows us to visualize and practice the dimensional change in each wave.

FOCUS

We must not forget the power of focus. Where is the dancer focusing his or her eyes? The focus of the eyes allows us to go into the mood, attitude, inner meaning of the dancer's work.

Try this simple exercise and study the changing moods of eye focus in relationship to body direction. For example,

Walking forward, eyes down
Walking backward, eyes up
Walking sideways to the right, looking right
Walking sideways to the left, looking right

The above examples will give you, as an observer, an important view of focus and how focus changes our visual understanding of what the movement or movements say to us.

Eye focus lends concentration, control, sincerity, and motivation to movement. The dancer can focus in many ways:

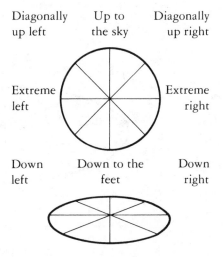

Diagonally up left — Up to the sky — Diagonally up right
Extreme left — Extreme right
Down left — Down to the feet — Down right

Practice looking in these various directions. The directions give us some relative location to the head. The head when twisting back over the right shoulder, and so on, has other directional innuendoes.

We could carry all directions to extremes, but the wonderful aspect of analyzing is that we can begin to understand where we are in space relative to the body and its parts, the floor, the space—vertically, horizontally, and dimensionally.

Dance is a three-dimensional experience, moving through many planes, creating many different shapes in axial and locomotor movement, and combining the two at such rapid pace that we can barely separate them. The space, the time, and the energy of movement exist in constant and direct relationship one to another. We separate them for sake of analysis, yet they are interrelated in every way.

EXPLORING AXIAL SPATIAL DESIGN

Space can be explored in many ways. One way is to recognize ourselves as the center of our own circle in space. The circle was selected because it contains all the degrees necessary to understand all sides of the body as it moves around itself in an axial spatial design.

The idea of centering ourselves in the middle of the circle implies that we understand the circumference of those 360° available to us, using a fixed base. We are then able to make a variety of choices in space.

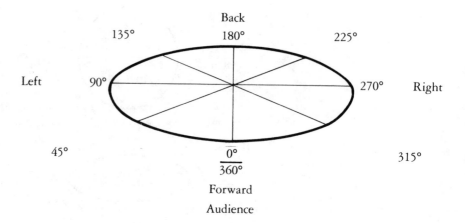

When traveling through space we still carry those 360° around us as we are moving a design in space. We are a moving body always changing, always moving in a degree of a spatial design even if we temporarily choose one degree and pursue that angle for a period of a few seconds or more. For example, this dancer is shown moving diagonally downstage left on the 315° diagonal; her right leg is diagonally upstage right at 135°.

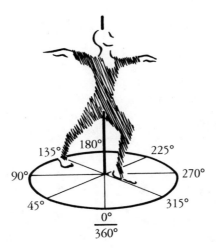

We constantly carry that circle with us and are capable of redirecting a design angle or degree of change at any moment.

The idea behind the 360°-circle concept is to allow ourselves a way in which we can locate ourselves in space directionally in terms of spatial angles.

EXPERIMENT 4

Space
PART 1: AXIAL SPATIAL DESIGN

Description   Part 1 is an experiment in knowing directional changes in space and identifying visually where we are in a 360° circle, that is, a 360° circle as it relates to an axial spatial design.

Problem   Create a solo study that moves around 360°. Remember, you are the center—front is 0° or 360°. Utilize at least six positions or moves to solve this directional problem.

Process   Study yourself inside a large circle. You may change level *(high, middle or low)*, but always be aware of where you are, for example, 180° to 0° to 45° to 280° and so on. Remember, 0° and 360° is absolute front; 180° is absolute back. You can begin and end in any chosen degrees.

Evaluation   Record on a circle with 360° the relative degrees of each move you have chosen. Repeat the sequences and see if the repeated movement coincides with the original statement.

In pencil, mark the circle on page 44 as a check chart to give validity in checking these specific degrees.

Using the 360° circle, describe the axial spatial design that each figure represents.

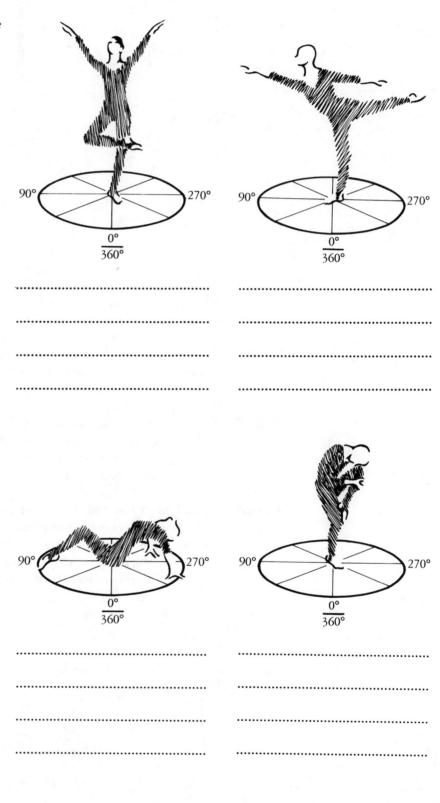

....

....

....

....

....

....

....

....

....

....

....

....

....

....

....

....

EXPLORING SPATIAL DESIGN

The human body is the natural form we work with when we create shapes in space.

The body in space can best be understood from these two points of view. First, the body lines can be seen as they occupy space. Second, you can see the space between the lines that the body makes in space, for example, the spaces between the legs, the arms, the head and the torso. Therefore, when we create with the body in space, we can see the form of the body as design. We can further identify the space the body occupies and the spaces between the lines of the various parts of the body as shown here.

Another example to enhance this understanding might include this description. A photograph of a dance position is a positive picture. The negative of that picture shows the opposite in terms of dark and light. Through this illustration we can see these specifics. The following figure on the left is dark and the space surrounding it is light. The dark area is positive space. The figure on the right is light and the space surrounding it is dark. On the right, the dark area shows negative space.

Positive

Negative

Positive space is the space that is occupied by a body, bodies, objects—the space occupied by something. Negative space is space that is unoccupied—the space where there is nothing. In the preceding illustration we can see how the body cuts space and how we form that space through the negative and positive process. Space is free; in this case we shape the space with the body. Your eye can see the body as a piece of formed sculpture (a held position). Your mind can also see and measure the various spaces that exist between the various parts of the body (the arms, head, legs and torso). Therefore, we will be concerned with the lines we make and the space we form between those lines. How we change the shape of the lines and the spaces between those lines helps us create new designs in space using the human form.

EXPERIMENT

Space
PART 2: SPATIAL DESIGNS

Description Part 2 is an experiment in designing the human form as a piece of sculpture in space.

Problem Create a solo study that moves in circular space using the 360° concept. Utilize twelve different body designs. Memorize, through your kinesthetic sense, where your arms, legs, head, torso, are facing. Be as accurate as possible. Your recall of positions is essential.

Process Using the space on the next page, draw stick figures to depict the shapes that you have created. Create twelve different shapes. Be able to successfully move and connect each shape to the next without your notes. Execute all twelve positions in slow motion moving through all twelve.

1

2

3

4

5

6

7

8

9

10

11

12

Evaluation Work in pairs to test each other's progress. Make concrete positive suggestions to assist your partner in mastering this sculptural concept in space. The following are suggested ideas to help you begin. Include your own and rearrange or repeat as desired.

1. Standing Design
2. Kneeling Design
3. Sitting Design
4. Lying Design
5. Reaching Design
6. Crawling Design
7. Sliding Design

8. ....
9. ....
10. ....
11. ....
12. ....

VARIATIONS

Take the twelve body designs and expand them in space, adding small sections of locomotor movements to connect each design (utilize the entire stage space). Change tempo and rhythms to add variety to these designed shapes. Through this process we can develop a sense of the body designs in space connecting with locomotor patterns moving through space.

SUGGESTIONS

Execute the above series of movements using a partner creating a duet in unison. Create any variations you wish, each having your own set of twelve designs and combinations.

An Experiment in Energy

≪ DYNAMICS ≫

Energy and the variations of the intensity of energy create the dynamic textures in dance movement. In the dynamics of energy we are concerned with the quality of movement. The qualities of movement are varied and they include the following: swinging, percussive, sustained, vibratory, suspended, and collapsing.

Swinging   *Swinging* is energy released with a pendular quality and can be accomplished in a variety of ways, for example, arms forward, backward, side-to-side, figure-eight with arms or arms crossing the body, parallel swings (both arms at the same time). Swings can be accomplished with the legs, the arms, the head, and the complete body if held by another person. Swings can be varied in so many ways using a head and an arm combination going into a leg swing, and so on. The combinations are many. Feel free to explore the possibilities and enjoy the outcome.

Percussive   *Percussive* energy is energy released in strong quick movements that result in a lot of force and stop. Karate is a good example of this type of strong hitting (for example, leg kicks or quick strong arm moves). Boxing is filled with percussive moves in hitting, punching, and generally releasing energy to create a strong force.

Sustained   *Sustained* movement is a continuous seemingly nonending motion. This continuous motion may be likened to a perfect plane ride at a high altitude—so smooth, so continuous, so unending. In dance movement the entire body may be involved. We may choose to isolate one body part and shift to another or include parts of the body.

Vibratory   *Vibratory* movement is quick-released body energy. The whole body can be involved or any body part can be isolated to project this kind of dynamic movement. Vibratory movement can cause exhaustion if pursued for too long. The use of this movement should be performed sparingly for effectiveness (for example, the flutter of hummingbird wings).

Suspended   *Suspended* movement is unique in that this action occurs when the force behind the action is held for a brief moment. This brief moment is suspended movement. When the suspended movement is performed accurately, it will cause the audience or onlooker to feel lifted as if you and the performer are being held for a moment in time. Suspending motion is exciting—it seems to defy gravity for a moment.

Collapsing   *Collapsing* movement is a natural fall whether completely to the floor or from any one of the parts of the body. A complete collapse is to the floor and melting into a relaxed feeling. The energy is freed and results in a form of giving in to gravity.

The dynamics of energy can refer to the movement qualities in dance. Also included in this area of dynamics is *intensity* and *accent*.

Intensity refers to the amount of energy used. Energy intensity ranges from the extreme of heightened energy relating to *tension* to the release of energy relating to *relaxation.* These two extremes give us the range of energy intensity.

An accent refers to increased or diminished force. The accent might include a sudden change in rhythm, level, intensity, movement quality, or emotion. In our understanding of energy an accent means a change—an application of energy differing from the movement preceding the accent. An accent is an emphasis. The most common accent definition in music and dance is an increase in energy.

EXPERIMENT 5

Energy
DYNAMICS

Description This is an experiment in blending various dynamic qualities into a small dance statement.

Problem Create a study with four dancers using four movement qualities: sustained, percussive, swinging, and vibratory (other movement qualities may be substituted for those utilized here, for example, suspended and collapsing).

Process There are four dancers, *A, B, C,* and *D. A* begins a statement using twelve counts of sustained movement without any accent. *B* begins after *A* has completed the statement and creates a twelve-count of percussive movement. *C* begins after *B* is finished and creates a twelve-count swinging statement. *D* begins after *C* is finished and creates a twelve-count vibratory statement. During the last set of twelve everyone—*A* sustained, *B* percussive, *C* swinging, *D* vibratory—dances their statements at the same time, showing these four dynamic moving qualities in contrast.

Evaluation Each set of four *(A, B, C,* and *D)* can match up with another set of four and dance their respective pieces of work for each other. They can check on counts, qualities of movement, and total work of the quartet.

Suggestions This study can be performed in front of a class. Also, the work can be doubled so that two sets of four display their work at the same time, making a total of eight people, yet displaying their work as two quartets. (The works can follow each other, or the works can be produced simultaneously). Each group of four has a total of sixty counts separately; as a group simultaneously, sixty counts; as a group following each other, a total of one hundred twenty counts.

Variations   The two quartets can choose to execute the total sixty counts of each other's group totaling one hundred twenty. Therefore, you would have Group 2 execute all of Group 1's work; then have Group 1 execute all of Group 2's work. The last statement could conclude with Group 1's work danced against Group 2's work. This shows unison work and then contrasting statements working against each other.

An Experiment in Concentration
≪ *LEARNING DETAILS* ≫

Concentration is the ability to keep our attention on one thing and sustain that complete involvement. This experiment is not easy since most of us will allow our energies to be changed from moment to moment. We can begin to get involved in the art of concentrating when we establish a common goal and then proceed to accomplish that goal as quickly as possible.

The following isolation exploration allows us to be selective and add another dimension to the understanding of movement.

EXPLORING CONCENTRATION

Freeze your own body in any standing position—now choose to isolate one part of your body as you execute the following. Experiment with these six areas. Allow ten seconds for each isolation. Flex the foot, rotate the hand, rotate the head, extend the leg, extend the arm, and then contract the torso. When this experiment is completed repeat until it is in your memory. This exploration allows us to find new areas in which we can develop movement. How we execute these isolations depends on each individual.

Concentration is important in our understanding of movement details while exploring isolations. When we concentrate on our own movement or on another person's movement, we can begin to look for details regarding movement and how that movement is executed.

Specific isolations are movements from any of the body parts can be utilized and isolated in a variety of ways such as rotation, flexion, contraction, extension, hyperextension, and so on.

Isolations force us to find new movement in special areas of the body.

EXPLORING ISOLATIONS

HEAD ....

SHOULDER ....

BACK ....

CHEST ....

ARM ....

HAND ....

ELBOW ....

HIPS ....

LEG ....

KNEE ....

ANKLE ....

FOOT ....

Find two different body part isolations and perform them simultaneously. Find movements that shift from one isolation to another, for example, shoulder rotation, head rotation, leg extension and foot flexion. Use the mirror to help you understand the isolations and arrange a series of isolations to fill fifteen seconds.

EXPLORING SPONTANEITY

Concentration can also be developed in an on-the-spot experience. First, think about what each of the following statements is asking you to do and note what each position will be. Work in pairs so that one is initiating the activity and the other is sight-reading (by observation only) the movement at the time of the experience.

1. Find a position called *A*.
2. Move slowly to a new position called *B*.
3. Move quickly in a position called *C*.
4. Run across the room, changing levels, and finish in position *D*.
5. Turn in slow motion; then quickly fall to the floor and end in position *E*.

Try this exercise the next time in unison.

CONCENTRATION RESULTS

1. The creator concentrates to create the initial experience.
2. The observer concentrates to see the whole, and senses the flow.
3. The second time through, the observer becomes the participant as well and concentrates this time to perform the work in unison.
4. If the work is learned, the creator can step back and watch the executed work now performed by the initial observer.
5. This repeatable performance is now accomplished when both creator and observer can perform the work in solo or unison.
6. A new statement can be made, using the same outline and having the observer become the creator and the creator become the observer.
7. The second time, make specific moves, utilizing flexions, extensions, rotations, and so on in the five-point experience. *Suggestion:* Develop specific body isolations in the body positions of A, B, C, D, and E.

By concentrating on movement isolations, we allow ourselves the privilege of growing rapidly and speeding up the creative process of discovery. *Fear* often forces us to slow up or limit the process. Each individual will concentrate according to his or her own ability, and will respond at different rates of speed in reaching the following objectives:

To open up to creativity

To allow discovery to be natural

To express oneself in simple, clear ways

To communicate with others without forcing

To create order out of disordered movement

To create ourselves anew as we develop

To sight-read movement with the beauty of understanding the kinesthetic sense

EXPERIMENT 6

Concentration
LEARNING DETAILS

Description   An experiment in understanding the value of learning movement details by visually concentrating on another person's movement pattern.

Problem   Follow the leader: create a study for two people using isolations, for example, foot, hand, torso, any body part, and manipulate these isolations any way you wish. One example is illustrated below.

Process   One person is *A* and the other person is *B*. Allow *A* to begin this series of movements using carefully spontaneous, on-the-spot movements and isolations. In this experiment, *B* is to follow *A* as closely as possible, reading the movement of *A*. Use about one minute. Then *B* is the leader and *A* follows for about one minute. Allow the spontaneous experience to exist as the leader leads, and the follower follows. Watch closely for details in movement.

Evaluation Each group of *A* and *B* will select another group *A* and *B*. They will help each other discover whether this intense concentration is taking place. Check on details to see if the isolations are being executed in unison. Group *A* and *B* can relate to each other as one. This relationship of intense concentration is acquired through the understanding of the details in the kinesthetic process.

SUGGESTIONS

The study can be shown in front of a group. When *A* leads, *B* follows. When *B* leads, *A* follows. (Use a timer with a stopwatch for each minute.) These studies can be new each time they are presented since they involve spontaneous, on-the-spot changes in movement.

7

An Experiment in Imagination Exploration
≪ *REALIZING SHAPES* ≫

Our own *imagination* is one of the keys to the success of our own creative process. We imagine through our thought process. This thought process projects various images into our conscious mind. Through our own brainstorming we ignite our mind and come up with spontaneous answers to questions, ideas, and visual images.

Our perceptual grasp of reality will give us clues to what we see in everyday life. For example, a diagonal line can be perceived as a hill. If we look at that line long enough we can imagine it to be a stick, a jet stream or anything we can imagine.

Another way to exercise or release our imagination is to actually take a walk and look for the diagonal line in our environment. We then can experience our imagination as a way of looking at everyday things; for instance, a diagonal crack in the sidewalk.

After we think about what we are trying to do we suddenly realize that our imagination helps us remember and perceive what we really see in life. Therefore, when we imagine, we actually put together new combinations in our mind and come up with rich images that are the keys to the creative process of imagination.

The imagination stimulates us to react to the world around us. When we look at visual shapes we begin to sense a relationship to those objects that exist for us in reality. As we visualize what we see in these shapes, we'll be exploring specific examples of our connections with our own individual thinking process. As a creation in dance, shape is important. How we look at shapes and how we use these shapes will help us connect these ideas into movement patterns, body designs, and forms that represent our ideas. Our imagination will continually be at work.

The imagination is constantly available to us. In this experiment the desire is to have each individual imagine what a shape represents while conjuring up various images for the three specific shapes. These shapes were selected to help individuals search for answers within their own set of experiences. The fill-in-the-blank approach leaves many choices for the creator to explore.

The second time through, each individual is asked to extend these forms into moving forms. The meanings here discussed will strengthen the ideas of movement and feeling states associated with them. After completing each section, a discussion should follow so that all members may have an opportunity to exercise and discuss their own imaginative ideas. The idea level is here even fantasized or clarified in one's imagination. The next phase is to structure a moving experience utilizing some part of several of these ideas.

IMAGINATION AND SHAPES

In the following exercise we will explore and discuss visual shapes. There are three shapes to think about; write down under each shape ten words or short phrases describing things you associate with each shape. For example, under the circle, perhaps write *sun;* under the triangle, perhaps *tepee;* under the diagonal, perhaps *staircase;* and so on. This exercise will help you visualize what each shape means to you.

◯	△	╱
1.	1.	1. ....
2.	2.	2. ....
3.	3.	3. ....
4.	4.	4. ....
5.	5.	5. ....
6.	6.	6. ....
7.	7.	7. ....
8.	8.	8. ....
9.	9.	9. ....
10.	10.	10. ....

In the next exercise, using the same three shapes, list what movements you can visualize that relate to these visual shapes. For example, for circle, perhaps *walking around;* triangle, *sliding* or *turning on the corners;* diagonal line, *running away from something;* and so on. Let your imagination stretch to find new meanings in shapes.

○	△	╱
1.	1.	1.
2.	2.	2.
3.	3.	3.
4.	4.	4.
5.	5.	5.
6.	6.	6.
7.	7.	7.
8.	8.	8.
9.	9.	9.

10. .... 10. .... 10. ....

    ....

11. .... 11. .... 11. ....

    ....

12. .... 12. .... 12. ....

    ....

EXPERIMENT

Imagination Exploration
REALIZING SHAPES

Description This is an experiment in creating visual designs in exploring space.

Problem Create a moving study by exploring the shapes of the circle, line, and triangle in space—first in solo, then in trio.

Process Create on a separate sheet of paper a series of moving designs, using the circle, triangle, and diagonal line. Concentrate on using these shapes only. By careful selection, identify what movement you want to include in each design. For an example, running in a circle, falling into a diagonal line, and slowly moving into a triangular walking pattern. You may become as simple or complex as you desire; however, limit your design to creating with these three shapes.

Evaluation Each individual, after completing this study, can work with two other people. This trio can then watch each other to see if they solved the problem, and give each other suggestions.

Suggestions The final statement can be shown in front of the group as solo statements. Another plan is to allow the trio to perform their work all at the same time, creating diagonals, circles, and triangles, occurring by chance. A very simple statement can then become a challenge to visually see these three pieces overlapping each other.

Variations Use other shapes such as squares, rectangles, two parallel lines, and so on and extend them into other movement designs and floor patterns.

An Experiment in Feeling Responses
≪ *HUMAN EMOTIONS* ≫

We can often miss our creative potential by losing the spontaneous feeling responses of our colorful selves. We grow up quickly and become quite controlled and conditioned.

When we begin to explore the human potential of our own feelings, we get in touch with the intuitive responses and those spontaneous feelings of our own childhood. As we establish a relationship to ourselves we begin to discover the importance of our own feelings. Our feelings motivate us to be expressive. Let us reflect on our own life experience and remember the value of our own emotional responses. List experiences that you have had as a child; both positive and negative feeling responses can be explored. Fill in the remaining spaces with your own thoughts.

1. Running with glee
2. Overturning a rock
3. Watching a ladybug
4. Fear of a dark place
5. Anger at being left out
6. Crying when being hurt
7. Laughing when you were silly
8. Jumping for joy

9. ....

10. ....

11. ....

12. ....

The beauty of these feelings can be discussed in a classroom situation. Identifying feelings and creating our own movement responses is the desire. We have already experienced these feelings in our past. We have temporarily relived them through our memory and discussion. The re-creation of these memories is a way of getting in touch with our feelings.

EXPLORING FEELINGS

Choose one idea from the list you completed. Select a beginning appropriate position. Now, through your own method, create movements to match your idea. (This experience can be spontaneous as in the act of improvised, on-the-spot movement). Your own movement habits give you your own individual character.

Create a movement sequence that is selective, using one of these ideas. Carefully choose movement that can create an expressive feeling state. You may choose to work from your own spontaneity and, through the act of improvisation (on-the-spot action), find movements that can be organized to form your idea.

Your chosen verbal phrase is your starting point. You can develop it in any direction you wish, using gestures, abstract movements, drama, or pantomime. If you make clear choices so you can relate to your idea, the audience will see your intention.

Human emotions are very important. They allow us the privilege to unite with the universal feelings of others and join in the celebration of life. Dance is concerned with the release of these human emotions in movement.

Emotions are a natural part of each person's life. Dance reaches for these feelings in self-expression. In order for us to be successful at self-expression in dance, we need to explore, discover, and observe feelings and shape our ideas to express ourselves in some meaningful moving form. On the most basic level, our outward expression, in the beginning, is primitive and simple. As we develop an awareness and sensitivity to ourselves and others we increase our ability to understand and deliver more complex ideas and feelings. Create a mental list of feelings that reflect the following moods and attitudes:

States of Tension	Release of Tension
Anger	Cozy
Crying	Comfortable
Suppressing	Sleeping

Hostility	Hanging Loose
Fear	Security
Anxiety	Peace
Tragedy	Comedy

....

....

....

....

....

....

....

....

....

Create your own inner dialogue about them and be able to discuss in a group situation after working and exploring these ideas in class.

Continually stimulate your mind by reflecting on feelings, and observe those feelings that exist in your everyday life. Also, look back into your own childhood, you own history, and think about the natural feelings you have experienced in your own life. Learn to connect your own thoughts about feelings that exist in your present and your past. Take notes to record the experiences you recall.

Here we are dealing with the happy and the sad; the comedy and the tragedy; the light and the dark side of human nature. We are interested in recognizing various human emotions and finding movement shapes and movement patterns to establish and clarify feelings of emotion. Knowing our own emotions, giving them form, and clarifying our movement meanings to say something is our purpose. When we study the extremes we will begin to see what makes the human emotions a strong source of movement.

EXPERIMENT **8**

Feeling Responses
HUMAN EMOTIONS

Description This is an experiment in understanding the various feeling responses and being able to identify two extremes.

Problem Create a solo or duet study that has the tension that exists in a negative emotion—for example, anger—then take an opposite positive emotion that releases that tension—for example, forgiveness or understanding— and show the contrast.

Process Study either your own emotions or those of your immediate family or friends. Carefully examine and be aware of the tensions that exist. Then be prepared to show the relaxation that follows either in a release or the replacing of another emotion. This study can be executed first in frozen form, such as a static position. Show the moment of anger as if it were a piece of sculpture. In slow motion, slowly move toward releasing that emotion and replacing it with a positive, more relaxed frozen sculptured position.

Evaluation The group may work with each other and observe the emotional extremes in pairs. Each person may show the other the set of emotions selected and formed. (The viewer and performer.) The viewer may give suggestions to the performer. The performer may accept or reject according to his or her perception of the criticism. Reverse the process and have the viewer perform his or her own work to be criticized.

 The motion of this study will be limited to a small space—for example, standing in one spot—and individuals will execute this work using limited, enlarged visual shapes or small diminutive ones when needed. *Caution:* do not overexaggerate! The study will deal with the essence of feeling being shown in a simple structural form.

Suggestions　After each individual has an opportunity to share with each other, allow selected solos to be performed before the group and make suggestions if needed to identify the emotions.

Variations　This study can be greatly enhanced by developing these emotional expressions into little dance pieces. Create situations in relationship between two people and develop the idea into a little statement, for example, two contented people, and then tragedy hits—the resolution may be comforting each other.

　　　　　　　Create a list of human situations and relationships and build on these emotional expressions. The beauty of the human spirit to relate to and create the human drama will enhance the thinking and feeling process of the dancers who are involved.

9

An Experiment in Making Connections
≪ *GESTURES* ≫

There are forms of dance that communicate by holding hands. They include folk and social forms. The initial gesture of holding hands generates the idea of connecting ourselves with other human beings. We feel secure when we know we are in touch with another human being. This sense of security is a statement often that we are one, that we are part of each other. Let's think about these human gestures and see what they reveal to us. When we touch, we begin to make connections to establish relationships of some kind—either short- or long-lived.

Shaking hands is that social connection saying I recognize that you and I are here together. We reach out to touch the other person to establish a connection and respond to their wholeness.

These movements allow us socially to touch another human being formally. When we touch, we feel; we sense the other person's energy; we now know the other person has also touched us. We have related to and have made the human connection.

In dance and in life, touching allows us the privilege of making that human connection possible by using gestures. One purpose of dance is to select meaningful movements and refine them until they form expressive ideas.

The human being has an instrument for immediate expression— it is his or her own body as a form of nonverbal communication.

The body can relate a variety of movements ranging from profound movements to trivial ones. All of our movements gloriously state, "Look—I am a human being in a body." This expression of reaching out to touch, clasp, hold, and so on is the human connection.

MAKING CONNECTIONS WITH YOUR HANDS

Complete the following list with your own creative suggestions concerning making the human connection, using your own hand, and another's. Complete the list to include your own ideas.

1. Shaking hands in a greeting.
2. Holding a hand to cross the street.
3. Touching a hand for comfort.
4. Clasping hands for courage.
5. Clapping your own hands in gratitude.
6. Reaching for a hand to share.
7. Holding hands in prayer
8. Touching a hand for an intimate moment.

9. ....

10. ....

11. ....

12. ....

13. ....

14. ....

15. ....

The exercise we have just completed gives us an opportunity to review the value of our human connections as they relate directly to our everyday life.

We have now reviewed the source and substance of *touching* to make the connection human.

GESTURES

Dance is filled with gestures projecting visible signs of bodily movement that reflect and relate to the simple or complex forms of daily communication. Our gestures are a form of human expression, and connection.

Fill in the blank spaces and list gestures to indicate other forms indicative of "making the human connection," either with or without touching.

1. Hug
2. Wave
3. Nod
4. Touch
5. Shoulder shrug

6. ....

7. ....

8. ....

9. ....

10. ....

11. ....

12. ....

13. ....

14. ....

15. ....

FROM NATURAL GESTURES TO ABSTRACT MOVEMENT

Gestures can be a basis for creative movement in dance. The desire in this case is to be able to make gestures and use the movement to communicate an idea in an abstract form. Gestures can be changed by making the movement larger or smaller or by changing the rhythm or dynamics of the gesture. The essence of abstract gestures can be seen and felt. The abstraction will help create the change from the natural into a new shape, a new way of looking at something old or making it uniquely new and unusual. The abstraction will create a fresh nuance or perhaps a new heightening of our senses. The ability to keep the essence and change the literal gesture into the abstract is the plan.

80

EXPERIMENT

Making Connections
GESTURES

Description   This is a lesson in discovering the human connections and applying these ideas to creative movements.

Problem   Solo or duet or a combination of a solo and duet. Create a dance movement study using two or more gestures that can include the movements of the human connection which involve touching and/or any other gestures as this example shows.

Process   Choose gestures that have meaning for you in your everyday experiences. Develop a small movement study that utilizes these gestures and expresses a simple idea. The study should include a beginning, a middle, and an end. (Time: About one minute.)

Evaluation   Evaluate yourself by writing down in words what you or you and your partner are trying to express. After completing your brief essay on what the small work was meant to say, do the following: Divide your group into twos if solos were designed; fours, if duets; and six if a solo and duets were the combination. Now, critically look at what each other has said and what was in fact accomplished in the movement sequence.

....

....

....

....

....

....

....

....

....

....

....

Suggestions   After everyone has had the opportunity to share and critique, allow selected works to be performed again in front of the group. Discuss the works performed and their success.

An Experiment in Improvisation

≪ *APPROACHES TO THE PROCESS* ≫

Improvisation is spontaneity in movement. Improvised movement can occur at any time, anywhere, and with anyone. Improvisation is a great part of our childhood play. We played under and over many objects. We searched. We discovered and we were free. We created our own freedom of expression with our spontaneous actions. We were characters in plays; we were objects; we experienced new highs and new lows. We imagined. We dreamed. We played out our desires.

All of the above approaches can be thought of as spontaneous, improvised movement. We often draw from our past to create the present. Sometimes our present creates our future. Regardless, we can be forever spontaneous. In improvisation we seek out our spontaneous person and ask for our self-expression in movement. Through improvisation, we can explore a variety of approaches in finding new movement sources for modern dance composition.

EXPLORING IMPROVISATION

Improvisation is the act of spontaneous, unrehearsed, instantaneous, fresh movement. This moving experience has an element of being uninhibited and totally free. In improvisation, the dancer has the opportunity to explore, to experience movement, and to let it all happen. A true freedom of expression exists for those involved in improvised studies. Improvisation is a happening in motion that you and others can create by chance. The ideas are numerous. Whatever you create is the choice you make when you improvise a movement. We improvise to find, investigate, make or experience new movement. Improvisation can be approached in many ways.

Improvisation can be created from word phrases. For example, add to this list.

1. Make me laugh
2. Show me
3. Be serious
4. I love you
5. It's a joke
6. Don't bother me
7. I am angry
8. Yes, I can
9. No, I can't

10. ....

11. ....

12. ....

13. ....

14. ....

15. ....

Improvisations can be created with objects. Add to the following list.

1. A volleyball
2. A large piece of fabric
3. An umbrella
4. Chairs
5. A ladder
6. A musical instrument

7. ....

8. ....

9. ....

10. ....

Improvisations can be created with music, rhythms, sounds. Add other sources of music, rhythms, and sounds to this list.

1. Drum beats
2. Traffic noise
3. The sound of birds
4. Any interesting piece of music

5. ....

6. ....

7. ....

8. ....

9. ....

10. ....

Improvisations can be created with dramatic ideas. Add to this list others that come to mind.

1. Two people meeting for the last time
2. Saying hello to a perfect stranger
3. Seeing an accident
4. Sharing a beautiful day or a rainbow with friends
5. Being surprised with a desired gift

6. ....

7. ....

8. ....

9. ....

10. ....

Improvisations might include recognizing various types of people and animals. Add others to these lists.

I am human
1. A child
2. An old man
3. A waitress

4. An entertainer
5. A clown

6. ....

7. ....

8. ....

9. ....

10. ....

I am animal

1. Tiger
2. Lion
3. Dog
4. Zebra
5. Lizard

6. ....

7. ....

8. ....

9. ....

10. ....

Now pair humans with animals from your lists.

1. A clown with a tiger
2. An old man with a dog
3. A waiter or waitress and a mouse
4. A child with a lizard

5. ....

6. ....

7. ....

8. ....

9. ....

10. ....

Improvisations can be solo, duet, trio, quartet, or a large group. Improvisations can be created with group situations and props. Add other combinations to this list.

1. Two people and one glass of water
2. Three people and two chairs
3. Four people and three brooms
4. Five people and one umbrella

5. ....

6. ....

7. ....

8. ....

9. ....

10. ....

Improvisation is an experience that is vital to any dancer. This process aids in the discovery, exploration, and experience of finding new movement for composition. When we are given an opportunity to work on improvisation we are given an opportunity to be original; no one can be you. Therefore, finding movement is essential in identifying your own power in creating. Taking charge of your creative self and asking for results is the discipline behind this spontaneous act of improvisation. Look forward to the self-discovery in movement exploration.

EXPLORING DRAMATIC SITUATIONS

Here is another list with situations which can be used dramatically. Make your choice and create an improvisation either solo or in a group of two or more. Perform the work in front of a class after you set up your given situation. First, add to the following list of dramatic situations.

1. Five people in a prison camp
2. Two people in a fire
3. Three people displaying vanity
4. Six people waiting in line
5. Five people all speaking different languages

6. Six people imitating a leader
7. Five people ordering food at once
8. Four people reading magazines at a newsstand
9. Four people eating sandwiches at a stand-up counter
10. Three people praying in a church
11. Four people in an earthquake
12. Three people in outer space
13. Five people late for work
14. One person walking on air
15. Three people at a class reunion

16. ....

17. ....

18. ....

19. ....

20. ....

The following list has a number of titles with suggested numbers of people beside them. The numbers can be changed or new titles added if desired.

The objective of this experiment is to find one that appeals to you and explore the idea as a solo performer or with a given group.

Enthusiasm	5 people (quintet)
Concentration	2 people (duet)
Images	3 people (trio)
Creativity	6 people (sextet)
Interaction	5 people (quintet)
Imitation	6 people (sextet)
Order	5 people (quintet)
Form	4 people (quartet)
Organization	4 people (quartet)
Simplicity	3 people (trio)
Focus	4 people (quartet)
Space	3 people (trio)
Time	5 people (quintet)
Energy	5 people (quintet)
Silence	1 person (solo)

EXPERIMENT 10

Improvisation
APPROACHES TO THE PROCESS

Description   This is an experiment in creating and performing an improvisational experience into a repeatable, small dance work.

Problem   Create a small dance work involving any of the choices of solo, duet, trio, quartet, or quintet selections.

Process   Choose a title and a group to stimulate a direct relationship to an improvised work. Make a list of words to create a feeling for the title. Find gestures that suggest the human connection. Create a series of movements that help develop the idea of the title.

Time   One to two minutes.

Space   Use predetermined shapes for the floor pattern such as diagonal lines, circles, or triangles, or create new ones if desired.

Energy   Use dynamics such as sustained, percussive, and so on to enhance your idea.

Evaluation   Be able to perform the created small work in front of an audience using spontaneous, improvised movement the first time through. Go back and spend some time and select improvised moments that give clues to the movement behind the title. See if you or your group can sense what part goes first, last, and what creates a middle. Create an order. Decide what is at the beginning, middle, or end.

Suggestions   Go over and over the remembered moments and establish a sense of remembered patterns. Encourage each person to start in unison, following one person, then another, to create a lot of spontaneity. Then, through discussion, find out what fits, where it fits, and what feels comfortable. You may need four or five drafts before a permanent orchestrated structure survives.

Perform this small work in front of another group to see whether your completed work has a sense of the title and a beginning, middle, and end. The work can evolve in a number of other ways. When the group feels satisfied with the results, perform the finished work before an audience.

An Experiment in Performance
≪ CREATING A COMPOSITION ≫

Modern dance is a unique form of self-expression. The human body is the source and substance of the dance. The dance is created by the dancer's own ideas using space, time, and energy. Dance is life itself in motion. The meaning in dance can be movement for its own sake or movement to express ideas, feelings, or any given moment in time.

Modern dance is a moving, ever changing form of self-expression, changing with each person and each generation. Modern dance is, philosophically, a part of declaring the importance of humans as individuals. We, as creators of dance, can enhance our view of life and the perceptions of our own feelings as we pursue dance.

Let us begin to discover our individual ideas in order to create a small dance. Ideas come from many places. Start by writing the history of your own life on two or three separate pages. After you have written your history, you will discover some of the varied aspects of your own life. Upon reflection, you will see that you have many things that can be selected as subject matter for a small dance composition.

Possible ideas may include in-depth feelings, short subjects, relationships, disappointments, memorable moments, or any comments on personal events, or movement for its own sake.

What do you, as a special person, want to say to yourself, to another individual, or group of people? Make a list of these ideas:

1. ....

2. ....

3. ....

4. ....

5. ....

6. ....

7. ....

8. ....

9. ....

10. ....

11. ....

12. ....

13. ....

14. ....

15. ....

This list of ideas can be a springboard to your creative composition. Some of the above ideas may be too grand for a small composition. Remember the more ideas you list, the more possibilities you create. Let's begin by selecting one of these ideas for a small composition. We want our first creative endeavor to be a personal success. We declare our success when we begin to work with our present abilities.

Our technical ability may be limited, or it may be far-reaching; regardless, we can establish some boundaries so that we can develop a jewel of a small composition.

First, find an idea from your list that you are familiar with, one that you yourself can believe in. Make a commitment to find sources for your movement that support your idea.

The real joy is to have an idea that will culminate in a small composed dance of your own creation. Selecting movement and organizing that movement into meaningful patterns is essential in the making of a dance. The dance is thereby controlled by our selection of these varied moving patterns. In creating the dance, there is the possibility the movement may be first, or perhaps the idea. The final product, the dance, will need a form.

FORMS

The dance composition you will be creating needs to have an overall shape, a form. The ability to organize your ideas and use movement to create a finished product is your aim.

The structure of your dance composition can be developed in a variety of ways. Here are some of the forms available to you as you develop your work: AB, ABA, theme and variation, rondo, round, and organic form.

AB The AB form has two parts, two contrasting statements. For example, the A may be twelve counts (locomotor). The B may be twelve counts (axial).

ABA The ABA form has three parts. The A is a statement involving one theme, and the B is a statement involving a contrasting theme. The A at the end represents a return to the original statement.

Theme and Variations (A_1, A_2, A_3, A_4, A_5) In the beginning of the theme and variations form, a theme is stated (a designed movement pattern). The theme ideally has a clear, recognizable shape in space. The variations on the theme can be developed in a variety of ways, changing rhythm, intensity, dynamics, and so on.

Rondo (ABACA, DAEA, etc.) The rondo form has a strong repetition of A repeated at least three times (it can, however, go on for a longer period). The A statement repeats over and over again as B, C, D, etc., is added to give and lend the unknown.

Round This form has a theme that repeats itself over and over again, introducing itself at equal distances so there is overlapping. For example,

A. **1 2 3 4 5 6 7 8**

B.   **1 2 3 4 5 6 7 8**

C.   **1 2 3 4 5 6 7 8**

D.   **1 2 3 4 5 6 7 8**

There are four individual groups; for example, each does the same eight counts. The first begins above the second. The theme is exactly the same each time it is danced.

Organic Form This form is developed in such a way that any or all parts are arranged according to one's own desire. You can repeat, add or subtract—anything you wish. You are free to choose.

MUSIC

Dance and music are partners. They are two strong individual components working together. The dancer must be aware of the overall rhythm and form; however, the dancer may choose to utilize going against the music or connecting with it as the dancer sees fit. The objective here is to avoid allowing the music to dominate the dance.

If you are fortunate and have a dance accompanist within the structure of the class, you can enjoy either having the accompanist improvise or have the work analyzed prior to the performance. The accompanist will then be able to find clues as to the rhythm, mood, and overall form and content of each individual work.

If you do not have an accompanist and you wish to have original music, you might try these alternatives: find a percussionist, flutist, pianist, or any musician who wishes to experiment with you. Insist that the music accompaniment augment your work. The music should not overtake the dance or destroy your intent. Rehearse your work beforehand, and if the results are satisfactory, utilize and enjoy your new artistic encounter and perform together.

Dance also can be performed in silence, with rhythmical devices, with voices sung or spoken. The potential for any accompaniment is limitless.

TITLE

Choose a title that belongs to your dance. Be selective and consider the content of your composition and how you want the work to relate to the audience. The title helps to describe to an audience what they will be seeing.

The name of your dance formally introduces your created work, no matter how small, to the audience. The title clues us in on your personal expression, on your dance.

AUDIENCE

The primary audience for the problem-solving experiments is the class itself.

If the class feels comfortable, a small studio performance may be given. The audience can be informed beforehand about the nature of the event. The audience can be given an introduction to what the projects include, and who the performers are (in this case they are beginning students). Therefore, when choosing an audience, the suggestion here is to include only those people invited by the students themselves, by invitation only.

THE DANCE COMPOSITION

The dance itself will need a beginning, a middle, and an end. The beginning and end are the shortest parts and must make a strong impression. You may compose the beginning first, the end first, or create a movement theme first; regardless, you need to start somewhere and begin to work.

Once you have planned a beginning, middle, and end, the parts must fit together tightly, like a finished jigsaw puzzle. The middle needs to develop your idea or movement theme. The time frame may be as short as a minute and a half, or as long as three minutes. We want to see something happening—a development—a statement.

Within the structure of the composition is a climax that may occur anywhere in the work—at the beginning, toward the middle, or near or at the end. The dramatic climax heightens our interest. The climax creates a built-in tension and intensity of feeling.

STATEMENTS ABOUT THE COMPOSITION

1. In a dance composition there is a *beginning,* a *middle,* and an *end* with a climax somewhere in the composition.
2. There is a *relationship* among the music (the accompaniment), the idea, and the dance statement.
3. There is a sense of *contrast* in the dynamic qualities, spatial designs, rhythms, etc.—a sense of texture.
4. The *parts* need to fit together like parts in a puzzle to create a wholeness—like a unified piece. A definite form (AB, ABA, etc.) can be followed or a free form can be developed.
5. Movement can be *repeated* so that the structure of the dance has the strength of overall design.
6. The *space* needs to be well defined in the performing area. The space that the dancer occupies and moves in needs clear body design, direction, focus, and pattern.
7. The *time* relationship between the dance or dancers needs to be clear, in unison, in counterpoint, in syncopation, etc. The rhythm structure of dance and music must be unified, directly contrasted, or used with some connected element; it could be background music to a dramatic, motivated idea.
8. The varied *energy* levels need to be present. How was energy used to create intensity and dynamic changes within the structure of the work?
9. *Concentration* is an essential element in projecting the sincerity

of the performed work. Concentration creates the intensity and involvement.

10. *Communication* occurs when you as a dancer understand the composition, and deliver something—a happening, a statement that is sequentially knitted together. The dancer says something nonverbally, and if the viewer receives the work, a communication occurs and the moving dialogue is translated as a new experience for the observer. The intended dance work is then received, to be accepted or rejected.

THINGS TO THINK ABOUT WHEN GETTING READY FOR A SMALL COMPOSITION AND PERFORMANCE

DEVELOP an awareness and a sensitivity to your surroundings and the space you will be dancing.

LEARN to appreciate your own unique way of moving and be confident.

ENJOY and *ANALYZE* what you are doing. Be well-rehearsed.

PROVOKE your own critical judgment of your work.

BE AWARE of the nature of your audience (your classmates). *ENJOY* the experience of performing for yourself as well as for others.

RECOGNIZE the characteristics of various individuals and/or groups of people that surround you. Face your fears and be courageous.

TALK TO and *ENCOURAGE* other dancers. Find out how they work and what they feel.

GAIN self-assurance.

The above statements are listed in order to face the anxiety present in the dancer, before and after the event of a small performance. Identifying the fears and sharing your feelings with others will reassure you that you are not alone.

The caring and sharing of the experience of the dance and dancers is an important aspect in educational dance. We are here together to discover and appreciate our efforts in self-expression.

EXPERIMENT 11

Performance
CREATING A COMPOSITION

Description This is an experiment in creating a small dance composition.

Problem Create a composition using any of the forms such as AB, ABA, round, organic, etc. Develop an idea that can be expressed in a time frame of a minute and a half to three minutes. Utilize no more than five dancers.

Process Find an idea you or others want to express. Select dancers who can perform the idea or movement. Begin with a brief written outline of what you or others want to accomplish. Bring in pre-designed movement, or choreograph the work together either through improvisation or highly structured dance counts. Begin by deciding what movement is done in unison; what movement is executed alone, or any combination as outlined. The following examples are possible combinations of movement patterns from solo to quintet.

solo	1 movement pattern
duet	2 or 1 + 1
trio	3 or 2 + 1 or 1 + 1 + 1
quartet	4 or 3 + 1 or 2 + 2 or 2 + 1 + 1 or 1 + 1 + 1 + 1
quintet	5 or 4 + 1 or 3 + 2 or 2 + 2 + 1 or 2 + 1 + 1 + 1 or 1 + 1 + 1 + 1 + 1.

These combinations can be helpful in designing the idea as well as the stage area. Then decide who will dance with whom, when, where, and how. Run through and check out a rough draft of the plan. You can arrange and change anything in any sequence you wish, but make sure everyone can count and is able to sense the concept or the idea and the overall form.

Refine your ideas as you go along, making sure each time the work is tighter and tighter until there are no loose ends. Everyone alive composes and approaches a dance uniquely in their own way. Review the checklist on composition for suggestions. Select title music and costumes that are basic to your idea.

EVALUATIONS

Each group can perform for another group and have their specific pieces critiqued personally by the group watching. Take the comments seriously and decide for your own group which comments seem to ring true. Evaluate your work; go back and clean up anything that seems inappropriate. Rehearse, believe in what you are doing, and enjoy the brief performance before the entire class.

An Experiment in Evaluation
≪ *APPRECIATING PROBLEM-SOLVING WORKS* ≫

Every day we evaluate our progress. We accept or reject our own development. We judge and misjudge. We understand and we are understood. We accept, and then we celebrate. There is a vast range of human emotions involved in the creative process. Do not be confused or discouraged by these extremes. Our goal is to create dance, using movement to give rise to a moving form of expression.

There are simple guidelines outlined below to help you develop, to be conscious, to be aware and to be concerned about evaluating the adventures of the dance. Evaluation is always difficult. View your work in the spirit of growth and constructive criticism. As you view your own and others' compositions, ask yourself these questions:

What did the dance composition express?

Did the movements express the idea?

How was space shaped?

How was energy utilized?

How was time used?

What form did the composition take? AB? Rondo? Something else?

In the final evaluation of other people's work or your own, ask yourself these questions:

Did the person or persons display confidence and sustain concentration?

Did the performers know where they were going?

Did you relate to their movement ideas?

Was the movement large or small; significant or insignificant?

Was there a sense of a beginning, middle, and end in the movement statement?

Was the work too long?

Was the work too short?

Were the movement statements interesting?

Did the work hold your attention?

Did you experience a positive or negative response?

Did the title relate to the dance?

Did the music enhance the dance composition?

Were the elements of contrast, repetition, and unity in evidence?

A SELF-EVALUATION

Be honest about yourself. After your performance ask yourself these questions:

1. *Were you committed to a level of quality in your work? Did you do your best?*

....

....

....

2. *Were you aware of your own improvement?*

....

....

....

3. *Were you consistent in your level of interest throughout your presentation?*

....

....

....

4. *Were your ideas linked to reality in any way?*

....

....

....

5. *Were you aware of your personal struggle?*

....

....

....

6. *Were you a contributor to the success of yourself and others?*

....

....

....

EXPERIMENT

Evaluation
APPRECIATING PROBLEM-SOLVING WORKS

Description An experiment in creating a way to evaluate a small work or experiment and appreciate the development of the performers.

Problem Create your own way of analyzing what you and others have accomplished in a small dance work or experiment.

Process Create in the space below a list of important questions that you and others can answer in order to evaluate and appreciate the dance. Make your questions your own.

....

....

....

....

....

Take the time to reflect on your own personal feelings and growth in watching yourself and others develop in performing in the preceding experiments.

Evaluation

How do you judge yourself? What were your demands?

....

....

....

....

....

....

Suggestions   Have a group discussion to understand what you and others have acquired and admired as a result of solving creative, moving problems. Ask yourselves what you accomplished? Share your personal discoveries and appreciations as well.

PART THREE
A Reflection

Self-Value and Self-Evaluation

We have been made aware of our own movements as a source of personal expression through creative problem-solving experiments. We have experienced and explored movement using the kinesthetic sense as a means of expressing various feeling states and spatial relationships. We have begun to identify with ourselves kinesthetically and have been given the time to experience the self as a moving force, using gestures to indicate moods and attitudes. We have explored feelings that reflect both the negative and the positive. We have begun to relate to ourselves as a creative, perceptive being, integrating ourselves with expressions that relate to our everyday world.

Finally, we have been relating to others in a patient, open atmosphere, developing confidence, appreciation, respect, and courage. The value of the dance experience includes quality learning using discipline and patience to experience the joy of controlling movements. These natural movements can then be appreciated for the subtleties in expression.

Self-value and self-evaluation is achieved by respecting the problem-solving method as an approach to self-discovery in movement. The self is further enhanced in performance of a small work in front of an audience. This performance allows all of us the privilege to share in the process of constructive criticism.

We then have shared in the experience that movement can be a source and means of communicating through dance. We have begun to see and understand the kinesthetic sense at work.

THE CREATIVE IMPULSE

Throughout these experiments the creative impulse has been manifested through numerous dance experiences. Now let us concentrate on the inner dialogue that accompanies our creative work in dance.

The following outline was designed to evoke questions and evaluate how the process has worked for you. These nine points can be used at any time for any lessons. Here we take the time to examine whether we have understood where we are in relationship to ourselves and our own work, whether in delivered lessons, projects, small works or larger works. This is a method to test our own awareness of the work created.

These nine points are directly related to create a self-examination process in order to coach ourselves into attaining a high level of quality and achievement. This review outline is a never ending process. We can stimulate our growth by reflection.

CREATIVE PROBLEM-SOLVING
A REVIEW OUTLINE

1. Understand the kinesthetic sense.
2. Discover the self and the imagination.
3. Find the channels for creative movement.
4. Overcome the fears in the creative process.
5. Gain knowledge of space, time, and energy.
6. Deliver the work through disciplined understood movement.
7. Perform the work with commitment and concentration.
8. Make the human connection with the performers and the audience.
9. Be aware and open for critical judgments.

CREATING THE INNER DIALOGUE

The act of creativity has never been easy, but who said it would be? However, we can assume that all of us have the potential for creative activity, yet most of us do not explore creativity as such for two generally popular reasons: fear and failure. Therefore, creativity has often been stopped.

Let's look at these two reasons and reflect on them. There is a fear of reaching for the unknown and risking a part of ourselves. This is a valid reason, yet not strong enough to stop us from exploring and experiencing the adventure of the unknown. How can we overcome this penetrating fear that stops us from going forward? The beginning of conquering fear is confronting that feeling within ourselves and allowing it to surface, and then taking the time to look at it. Fear diminishes when we replace it with a positive action. In this case, the positive action is trying. Trying for the unknown leads us into new areas of discovery.

The popular second reason that exists comes from that of experiencing the feeling of failure. We may fail, but if we reach out and discover that negative emotion we can stretch and win over ourselves when we accept that eventual joy of discovery by *allowing* ourselves the privilege to experiment. When we experiment, we must include the right to fail before we succeed. Many scientists, artists, athletes, and explorers have experimented and failed numerous times before they reached even a small iota of success.

So often in our instant society we feel success must be immediate—even in creativity. This demand by society for instant success leads us to feel insecure because we think we must succeed on the first try.

Finally, when we conquer fear and failure we can still feel vulnerable and insecure because of possible criticism. Criticism is essential, for it is our guide to further discovery. Positive, constructive criticism destroys negativity and destructive tendencies, and leads to a growing creative atmosphere which is essential for every person who is creating.

These thoughts on fear, failure, insecurity and criticism in creativity have often stopped people with creative potential. As a result, many people have not experienced the ecstatic discovery and excitement in creating something new and something that personally belongs to them. Be a creator, for it is in pursuing creativity that creativity grows.

THE INNER DIALOGUE: MOTIVATIONAL THOUGHTS

A strange phenomenon keeps happening when one spends hours each day working to solve problems and finding solutions along the way. The phenomenon, in this case, is the inner dialogue that enhances your own relationship to yourself. Do not underestimate the power or the beauty available to you as you explore your own depths.

Each day you will have another part of the combination in understanding the full spectrum of color and action in unlimited ideas. The objective is to catch how you think, feel, or react. Keep a written record to stimulate your own progress. You may choose to write in a personal diary. Create your own supportive relationship with yourself. Use pen and paper to contact your innermost thoughts as you work through your day-to-day problem-solving experiences. The insights you gain about yourself and others can help you grow creatively as your inner dialogue increases.

My personal choice has been to isolate certain creative thoughts, which I, as someone who is also in search of the creativity within, would like to share with you. The following special creative thoughts may help you to stimulate your own creative inner dialogue.

Creativity
A creative attitude is a way of life open to change, constant risk, discovery, growth, and adventure.

Create to discover.

Creative living is an aim of our existence.

To be creatively alive is magical.

Our creative hands can produce the God-like genius of applied talent.

One who practices these virtuous gifts of talent maintains the harmony and flow of beauty that is found in the creation.

The will to do—the will to create—is the will to motivate creativity.

Life
Give to life—it's the best investment.

Drop the self-conscious to be human-conscious—conscious of feeling, sensing the moment and relating to it without fear of failure.

Faith is a bond within the spirit of people to say we will respond.

If we realized that every action sets our destiny in motion, oh! how conscious we would be.

Aesthetics
Beauty has many stages—we are but one.

Human Emotions
With expression, joy exists; without it, there is only a void.

Without words the silence grows strong as strength rises to the surface of your face.

And sorrow like a big wave comes forth—as if from nowhere—and pulls away.

The glance of an eye dispels despair.

Education
Determination is an exciting element in learning.

Vitality is exercising feelings—getting to know them.

Personal dissatisfaction often leads to success.

Inspiration
All inspiration has the spirit within.

Knowing how to release the spirit within and giving it out is life.

The form will be seen—seen in people—but it's the unseen that will be truly felt.

Glossary

Accelerando	Gradually increasing the speed in time.
Accent	Increase in stress or intensity in the movement.
Adagio	Slowly, in a graceful manner.
Allegro	Quickly, in a brisk manner.
Andante	Moderately slow.
Asymmetrical	Lack of balance, as in an unbalanced design.
Awareness	An alert, conscious response.
Axial	Nonlocomotor; characterized by movement that occurs around the central axis of the dancer's body.
Beat	The underlying constant pulse or count in music that divides the music mathematically; for example, $\frac{3}{4}$ indicates three beats per measure, $\frac{4}{4}$ indicates four.
Character	A person in a play, novel, or dance.
Closure	The end; the finish that makes a work complete; the closing.
Collapsing	Releasing the energy of a part of the body, or entire body so that it reaches a relaxed state.
Commitment	The state of being intellectually and emotionally dedicated to work.
Communicate	To impart; to give or exchange feelings or ideas.
Compose	Literally "to put together"; to create into a form.
Concentration	The act of focusing on an activity; being totally absorbed with the activity.
Conception	An original idea or design originating in the mind.
Connect	To join at least two things together.

Contrast To compare elements that differ from one another—to set them side by side—to show their dissimilar qualities.

Creativity The ability to put things together with imaginative expressiveness and originality.

Crescendo With an increasing tempo, intensity, or volume.

Cumulative rhythm A rhythm pattern that increases by using progressive additions; for example, 1, 1–2, 1–2–3, 1–2–3–4, 1–2–3–4–5.

Decrescendo With a slowly decreasing tempo, intensity, or volume.

Diminuendo *See* Decrescendo.

Direction The imaginary line leading to a place one is moving toward.

Discipline Strict self-control.

Discover To find out something—either new or old—for the first time.

Duet A composition for two instruments or voices; a dance for two persons.

Dynamics The amount of various energies used in movement with regard to changes of intensity, varying qualities, and accents.

Energy Power, or the amount of intensity in the movement.

Enthusiasm The state of being eager and interested.

Experience Prior knowledge achieved by living through an event.

Experiment To test out and discover new ways.

Evaluate To judge or find value in something.

Fast Quick or swift, as in movement.

Feeling Experiencing an emotion; being aware of being sad, happy, angry, etc.

Focus The direction of the movement in terms of the performer's eyes on a fixed point in space that can change with the performer's intent.

Form A structure; a shape.

Gesture The movement of the limbs or body to express a thought, feeling, or sensation.

Image A mental picture or a visual impression.

Imagine To conceive of in the mind.

Imagination The process of forming many images or making new creations.

Imitate To follow and be like in action, attitude, or form.

Impetus Energy released to begin a movement.

Impulse The desire to act or move forward.

Insight To see through intuition or an inner understanding.

Intensity	Amount of energy used in a movement; the lesser or greater degree of power.
Interaction	Action between individuals or groups.
Kinesthesia	The inner body awareness of movement in relation to space, energy, and size of movement; a sense of movement internalized by the muscles through nerve endings within the structure of the body; a sense of knowing where you are in space in relation to yourself.
Legato	In a way that is smooth and even.
Locomotor	Characterized by movement that travels through space; for example, walking, running, hopping, skipping, jumping, galloping, and leaping.
Memorize	To learn to recall on command.
Meter	The structure used in music to indicate the number of beats in a measure, represented by the time signature; for example, $\frac{3}{4}$ or $\frac{6}{8}$.
Moderato	In a moderate tempo.
Motion	To make a gesture to move into another position; to move any part of the body.
Negative	Opposed to the positive.
Notes	A written record to help the memory.
Order	A plan or a method; an arranging into positions.
Organic form	Organized, but in a natural way.
Organize	To arrange; to provide structure.
Percussive	Characterized by energy released in quick time actions; action that starts and stops sharply.
Positive	Confident and constructive.
Quartet	A group of four dancers, musicians, or other performers.
Relaxation	To rest; to become less tense.
Retard	A slowing of the rate of speed.
Risk	To expose oneself to chance.
Score	To keep a record; to record how a series of movements develop.
Select	To choose a specific movement.
Share	To give to others.
Silence	Being still; making no movement.
Simple	Plain, natural.
Slow	Characterized by motion taking a long time in executing each movement.
Solo	A performance by one person.

Space	That area where all things are contained; the distance or area between things.
Speed	The rate of movement.
Staccato	Characterized by short, sharp, crisp attacking movement.
Subito	Immediate; sudden and quick.
Suspended	Characterized by energy held for an instant in space, creating an illusion of resisting gravity.
Sustained	Characterized by energy held with a continuous feeling of no beginning, no middle, and no end; very controlled.
Swinging	Characterized by energy released as a pendulum does.
Symmetry	The state of both sides of equal parts in balance, structure and design.
Tempo	The rate of speed relative to movement, either fast, slow, moderate, or some other variation.
Tension	Stress exerted to produce a pull of force causing an extension or contraction.
Time	The period in which something happens.
Time signature	The mathematical fraction—the meter—preceding the measure to indicate how time is divided in that measure.
Timing	The speed to achieve the most effective performance.
Trio	Three performers in a composition.
Unison	The state of performers performing the same part.
Vibratory	Characterized by energy quickly released over and over again (like a body tremor).
Visual	Able to be seen.
Work	Physical and mental activity directed toward the production or accomplishment of something.

Bibliography

Anderson, Jack. *Dance.* New York, New York: Newsweek Books, 1974.

Arguelles, Jose, & Miriam Arguelles. *Mandala.* Berkeley, California: Shambala Publications, Inc., 1972.

Arnheim, Rudolph. *Art and Visual Perception.* Berkeley, California: University of California Press, 1972.

———. *Toward a Psychology of Art.* Berkeley, California: University of California Press, 1962.

Bruner, Jerome. *On Knowing: Essays for the Left Hand.* Cambridge: Harvard University Press, 1962.

Carpenter, Edmund. *They Became What They Beheld.* New York: Ballantine Books, Inc., 1970.

Chujay, Anatole and P.W. Manchester (ed.) *The Dance Encyclopedia.* New York: Simon and Schuster, 1967.

Collingwood, R. G. *The Principles of Art.* New York: Galaxy Paperback GB11, 1963.

Copland, Aaron. *Music and Imagination.* Cambridge: Harvard University Press, 1952.

Crip, Clement, and Mary Clarke. *Making A Ballet.* New York: Macmillan Company, 1974.

DeMille, Agnes. *The Book of Dance.* New York: Golden Press, 1963.

———. *To a Young Dancer.* Boston: Little, Brown and Company, 1962.

Dewey, John. *Art as Experience.* New York: Capricorn Books, 1958.

Duncan, Isadora. *Art of the Dance.* New York: Theatre Arts, Inc., 1928.

Ellfeldt, Lois. *A Primer for Choreographers.* Palo Alto, California: National Press Books, 1967.

Ellfeldt, Lois. *Dance From Magic to Art.* Dubuque, Iowa: William C. Brown Co., 1976.

Ellfeldt, Lois, & Edwin Carnes. *Dance Production Handbook; or, Later Is Too Late*. Palo Alto, CA: National Press Books, 1971.

Ellis, Havelock. *The Dance of Life*. New York: The Modern Library, 1929.

Fuller, Buckminster. *Ideas and Integrities*. Toronto, Ontario, Canada: Macmillan Company, 1969.

Gates, Alice A. *A New Look at Movement—A Dancer's View*. Minneapolis, Minnesota: Burgess Publishing Company, 1968.

Ghislin, Brewster. *The Creative Process*. New York: Menton Paperback, 1958.

Gilbert, Pia, & Lockhart, Aileene. *Music for the Modern Dance*. Dubuque, Iowa: William C. Brown Co., 1961.

Hawkins, Alma. *Creating Through Dance*. Englewood Cliffs, New Jersey: Prentice-Hall, 1964.

Hayes, Elizabeth R. *Dance Composition and Production for High Schools and Colleges*. New York: The Ronald Press Company, 1955.

H'Doubler, Margaret N. *Dance: A Creative Art Experience*. Madison, Wisconsin: The University of Wisconsin Press, 1959.

Humphrey, Doris. *The Art of Making Dances*. New York: Holt, Rinehart and Winston, 1959; Grove Press, 1962.

Jung, Carl G. *Man and His Symbols*. New York: Dell Publishing Company, Inc., 1973.

Karshan, Donald. *Conceptual Art and Conceptual Aspects*. New York: The New York Cultural Center, 1970.

Kochno, Boris. *Diaghilev and the Ballet Russe*. New York: Harper and Row, Publishers, 1970.

Kraus, Richard, & Sarah Chapman. *History of the Dance in Art and Education*, 2d ed. Englewood Cliffs, New Jersey: Prentice-Hall, Inc., 1981.

Krokover, Rosalyn. *The New Borzoi Book of Ballets*. New York: Alfred A. Knopf, 1956.

Laban, Rudolf. *The Mastery of Movement on Stage*. London: MacDonald and Evans, 1950.

Langer, Suzanne K. *Feeling and Form: A Theory of Art*. New York: Charles Scribner's Sons, 1956.

———. *Mind: An Essay on Human Feeling*. Baltimore, Maryland: The John Hopkins Press, 1967.

———. *Philosophy in a New Key*. New York: Mentor Books, 1951.

———. *Problems of Art*. New York: Charles Scribner's Sons, 1957.

———. *Reflections on Art*. New York Oxford University Press, 1961.

Lawson, Joan. *The Principles of Classical Dance*. New York, New York: Alfred H. Knopf, 1980.

Livet, Anne. *Contemporary Dance*. New York, New York: Abbeville Press, Inc., 1978.

Lloyd, Margaret. *The Borzoi Book of Modern Dance.* Brooklyn, New York: Dance Horizons, 1970 (reprint).

Lockhart, Aileene, & Esther E. Pease. *Modern Dance: Building and Teaching Lessons.* 6th ed. Dubuque, Iowa: William C. Brown Co., 1982.

Martin, Ben. *Marcel Marceau—Master of Mime.* United Kingdom: Pottington Press, Ltd., 1976.

Martin, John. *American Dancing.* New York: Dodge Publishing Company, 1936.

Martin, John. *Introduction to the Dance.* New York: Dance Horizons, Inc., 1965.

May, Rollo. *Love and Will.* New York: W. W. Norton and Company, 1973.

Mazo, Joseph H. *Prime Movers.* New York: William Morrow and Company, Inc., 1977.

McDonagh, Don. *Complete Guide to Modern Dance.* Garden City, New York: Doubleday & Co., Inc., 1976.

Meerloo, Abraham M. *Dance Craze and Sacred Dance.* London: P. Owen, 1962.

Metheny, Eleanor. *Connotations of Movement in Sport and Dance.* Dubuque, Iowa: William C. Brown Co., 1965.

Morgan, Barbara. *Barbara Morgan.* New York: Morgan and Morgan, Inc., 1972.

Murray, Jan. *Dance Now.* Middlesex: England: Penguin Books, Ltd., 1979.

Parker, DeWitt H. *The Principles of Aesthetics.* New York: Appleton-Century-Crofts, Inc., 1946.

Pease, Esther E. *Modern Dance,* 2d ed. Dubuque, Iowa: William C. Brown Co., 1976.

Penrod, James. *Movement for the Performing Artist.* Palo Alto, California: Mayfield Publishing Company, 1974.

Penrod, James, & Janice Gudde Plastino. *The Dancer Prepares: Modern Dance for Beginners,* 2d ed. Palo Alto, California: Mayfield Publishing Company, 1980.

Percival, John. *Modern Ballet.* Great Britain: Studio Vista Limited, 1980.

Radir, Ruth. *Modern Dance.* New York: A.S. Barnes and Company, 1944.

Read, Herbert. *The Forms of Things Unknown.* New York: The World Publishing Company, 1963.

———. *The Grass Roots of Art.* New York: Meridian Paperback, 1961.

———. *The Meaning of Art.* Baltimore: Penguin Books, Inc., 1950.

Rugg, Harold. *Imagination.* New York: Harper and Row Publishers, 1963.

Sachs, Curt. *World History of the Dance.* New York: W. W. Norton and Company, Inc., 1937.

Schlaich, Joan, & Betty DuPont. *Dance: The Art of Production.* St. Louis: The C.V. Mosby Company, 1977.

Shahn, Ben. *The Shape of Content.* New York: Vintage Books, 1957.

Sherbon, Elizabeth. *On the Count of One: Modern Dance Methods,* 3d ed. Palo Alto, CA: Mayfield Publishing Co., 1982.

Shurr, Gertrude, & Rachael Dunaven Yocom. *Modern Dance: Techniques and Teaching.* New York: The Ronald Press Company, 1949. (also *Dance Horizons* reprint, 1980).

Sorrell, Walter. *Dance in Its Time.* Garden City, New York: Anchor Press, Doubleday, 1981.

Stanislavski, Constantin. *An Actor Prepares.* New York: Theatre Arts, Inc., 1936.

Terry, Walter. *Dance in America.* New York: Harper and Brothers, 1956.

———. *Invitation to the Dance.* New York: A.S. Barnes and Company, 1942.

Van Praagh, Peggy. *The Choreographic Art.* New York: Alfred A. Knopf, 1963.

Wigman, Mary. *The Language of Dance.* Middletown, Connecticut: Wesleyan University Press, 1966.

Willis, John. *Dance World.* New York: Crown Publishers, Inc., 1971.

Winters, Shirley J. *Creative Rhythmic Movement.* Dubuque, Iowa: William C. Brown Co., 1975.